Homespun Remedies

by the same authors

Yoga for Children with Autism Spectrum Disorders
A Step-by-Step Guide for Parents and Caregivers
Dion E. Betts and Stacey W. Betts
Forewords by Louise Goldberg and Joshua S. Betts
ISBN 1 84310 817 8

of related interest

Kids in the Syndrome Mix of ADHD, LD, Asperger's,
Tourette's, Bipolar, and More!
The one stop guide for parents, teachers, and other professionals
Martin L. Kutscher MD, with contributions from Tony Attwood PhD and Robert R. Wolff MD
ISBN 1 84310 810 0 hb
ISBN 1 84310 811 9 pb

Parent to Parent
Information and Inspiration for Parents Dealing
with Autism or Asperger's Syndrome
Ann Boushéy
ISBN 1 84310 774 0

Parenting Across the Autism Spectrum
Unexpected Lessons We Have Learned
Maureen F. Morrell and Ann Palmer
ISBN 1 84310 807 0

Parenting a Child with Asperger Syndrome
200 Tips and Strategies
Brenda Boyd
ISBN 1 84310 137 8

Raising a Child with Autism
A Guide to Applied Behavior Analysis for Parents
Shira Richman
ISBN 1 85302 910 6

Achieving Best Behavior for Children with Developmental Disabilities
A Step-By-Step Workbook for Parents and Carers
Pamela Lewis
ISBN 1 84310 809 7

Encouraging Appropriate Behavior for Children on the Autism Spectrum
Frequently Asked Questions
Shira Richman
ISBN 1 84310 825 9

Homespun Remedies

*Strategies in the Home and Community
for Children with Autism Spectrum
and Other Disorders*

Dion E. Betts, Ed.D. and Nancy J. Patrick, Ph.D.

Jessica Kingsley Publishers
London and Philadelphia

First published in 2006
by Jessica Kingsley Publishers
116 Pentonville Road
London N1 9JB, UK
and
400 Market Street, Suite 400
Philadelphia, PA 19106, USA

www.jkp.com

Library of Congress Cataloging in Publication Data
Betts, Dion E. (Dion Emile), 1963-
 Homespun remedies : strategies in the home and community for children with autism
spectrum and other disorders / Dion E. Betts and Nancy J. Patrick.
  p. cm.
 Includes bibliographical references.
 ISBN-13: 978-1-84310-813-9 (pbk. : alk. paper)
 ISBN-10: 1-84310-813-5 (pbk. : alk. paper) 1. Autism in children. 2. Autistic
children--Education. I. Patrick, Nancy J. (Nancy Jo), 1955- II. Title.
 RJ506.A9B45 2006
 649'.154--dc22

                                                     2005033504

British Library Cataloguing in Publication Data
A CIP catalogue record for this book is available from the British Library

ISBN-13: 978 1 84310 813 9
ISBN-10: 1 84310 813 5

Printed and bound in Great Britain by
Athenaeum Press, Gateshead, Tyne and Wear

My wife Stacey contributed greatly to the ideas in this book. She provided me with constant encouragement. This book could not have been written without her. She has taken a leave from her practice as an attorney to expertly care for our five children, the oldest of whom has Asperger Syndrome. I dedicate my contribution to this book to Stacey, whom I love dearly.

Dion E. Betts

I dedicate this book to my supportive and loving husband Bill and three children Craig, Scott, and Blair. They have sacrificed much over the years to allow me to pursue scholarly endeavors and service to others. Their enthusiasm for this particular project was the fuel that energized me to the finish line. I am eternally grateful for all of their support.

Nancy J. Patrick

Acknowledgements

We wish to thank the many parents with whom we have worked over the past twenty years. They have generously shared their stories about their lives and experiences with their children. They were honest about the frustrations and successes with children with autism spectrum disorders. Much of this book is our attempt to pass along the homespun remedies generated by these pioneers.

A note on the book

The information in this book is intended to be just one part in a comprehensive program of care for children with autism spectrum disorders that is provided by parents, caregivers, and educational, and medical professionals. The information in this book is not intended to "cure" these disorders. There is no cure for autism at this time. A medical examination by a physician for a child suspected of having an autism spectrum disorder and other possible disorders is essential.

Many children have additional medical problems in addition to their diagnosed autism spectrum disorder. Parents and caregivers are encouraged to consult with a physician before acting on some of the recommendations in this book.

Many of the stories in this book are based on the kinds of experiences that many families with children with autism spectrum disorders go through. Stories and recommendations are not based on word-for-word interviews. Rather, they are based on a culmination of the authors' experiences with children and families. Thus, any perceived depiction of actual individuals is purely coincidental.

Contents

Introduction: What is So Special about Children with Autism Spectrum Disorders?   9

What are autism spectrum disorders?   11

Experiences of children with autism spectrum disorders   11

What parents and caregivers need to know   12

How to use this book   14

1: Home Life   15

Babysitters 17; Bees 21; Breastfeeding 23; Discipline 25; Dogs 27; Finances 29; Food 32; Friendships 34; Holidays 36; Marriage issues 38; Mealtimes 40; Morning and nighttime routines 42; Noise 44; Organization 46; Preferences 48; Respite care 51; Restaurants 54; Siblings and other relatives 56; Support groups 58; Talking about disabilities 60; Tantrums 62; Telephone skills 65; Textures and temperatures 67; Weather 69

2: Hygiene   71

Bath time 72; Brushing teeth 74; Clothes 75; Grooming 76; Haircuts 78; Nail clipping 82; Toilet training 83

3: Community   86

Airplanes 88; Birthday parties 90; Car travel 92; Hotels and vacations 94; Play dates 95; Shopping 97; Shoe stores 99; Swimming pools 101; Visiting other families 103

4: Medical   105

Dentist and doctor visits 106; Emergencies 108; Emergency phone calls 110; Immunizations 112; Medications 114

5: Schools and Organizations   **116**

Breaks 117; Bus rides 119; Clubs 121; Evaluations 123; Hobbies 124;
Homework 126; Mental health agencies 128; Religious services 129;
Report cards 131; School lunches 133; School team meetings 136;
Sports: Hallie's story 138; Sports: John's story 140; Teacher assistants
142; Therapists 144; Valentine's Day 146

6: Tools for Adapting the Environment for Success   **147**

Behavior plans   147
Choice boards   148
Direct instruction   149
First-then statement cards   151
Macro and micro schedules   151
Role-playing   153
Scripting   154
Symbol communication systems   155
Task analysis   156
Wait boxes   157

Conclusion   **158**

References   **159**

Introduction: What is So Special about Children with Autism Spectrum Disorders?

Paula is now ten years old. She is a beautiful girl with long blonde hair and sparkling blue eyes. Her hair is lifted off her forehead by a cowlick just left of center, which gives her a fresh wind-blown look.

If you were to look at her in a photograph or watch her sleeping, you would think that she most assuredly would be a popular girl, maybe even the most popular girl in her class. I have often asked myself what makes a child popular among their peers or even allows them to make and keep friendships. I used to think that maybe it had something to do with the way you looked or the way you dressed, but I have come to learn that it is much more than that. My life with Paula has been a journey of getting to know my child, observing her living, seeing her struggles and then trying to create solutions for her deficits that would allow her to live a full and meaningful life.

I first realized that other children did not seem to warm to Paula when she was three years old. At that point, I made a concerted effort to have her attend playgroups, preschool, participate in soccer, and sing in the children's church choir. I was vigilant in getting reports from the people supervising each social encounter, so that I could repair any problem between Paula and the adults or children. Most of the infractions with adults had to do with her correcting them, which was interpreted as rude and sometimes defiant.

Most of the problems with the children involved insensitivity to their opinions and perspectives. This in many cases involved competing at inappropriate times, being bossy, not including their ideas in the playtime, and, in general, being quite self-centered. Occasionally

Paula would recognize a mistake or would acknowledge a cue from me that she had done something terribly wrong, but she did not know how to correct the problem on the spot to recoup the friendship, even when she had some awareness that a problem had arisen.

Over the years, the invitations to events and activities ceased. Other children occasionally responded positively to invitations to play, but even those play dates were infrequent. She still longed for friends even though almost every social situation ended on a negative note. Paula was far less distressed by the situations than her playmates. Paula begs for friends.

Finally, someone agreed to come and play with her. We talked about it. We planned. Paula and I previewed the day to ensure a successful event with the hope that this would be ongoing. The first thing she did was to compete with the child. Paula told her friend, "I bet I can swim across the pool faster than you can." She couldn't. Her friend looked at her, and was quiet and polite. She never called again.

Sarah, Paula's mom

Zach kept crying and yelling about having to come to dinner. He really freaked when I shut off the computer. He said, "You don't care about me, all you care about is the stupid dinner." I get him to sit for dinner and he sees that we are eating hotdogs. Zach cries and hits his hands on the table. My other kids yell back at him. Zach gets up to hit his brother. I say, "Ok, I'll make you some spaghetti." Zach then says he wants it with tomato sauce, not butter. I say okay. The other kids also want spaghetti now. The menu for everyone changed to spaghetti with tomato sauce. The hotdogs return to the refrigerator.

Frank, Zach's dad

Some people would say that these children are spoiled. However, their distress is real. It torments them and pervades all aspects of family life. This book is a collection of practical remedies for daily predicaments for children with autism spectrum disorders. It is a culmination of many families' experiences and their tried and true solutions to everything from bringing a child to the dentist to family vacations. What parents of children with autism spectrum disorders know is that their children are different. Many times they do not know why this is so. Parents and caregivers want to explain to friends and family why their child is different. They also want to know how to make the home and community more calm and joyful.

What are autism spectrum disorders?

Autism spectrum disorders are disorders of communication, social relatedness, and self-regulation. What may underlie autism spectrum disorders are atypical central nervous systems. There is disagreement among parents, practitioners, and researchers regarding the causes, diagnosis, and treatment of autism spectrum disorders. Moreover, there is a dispute as to how to differentiate between autism spectrum disorders in making diagnoses. Under the umbrella of pervasive developmental disorders are the disorders of: autism, Asperger Syndrome, Childhood Disintegrative Disorder, Rett's Syndrome, and Pervasive Developmental Disorder/Not Otherwise Specified (PDD/NOS). The Diagnostic and Statistical Manual of Mental Disorders (American Psychiatric Association 1994) outlines the diagnostic criteria for each of these disorders. Here we use the term autism spectrum disorder to refer to what are considered pervasive developmental disorders.

We do not intend to explore the controversy over the causes or specific methods of diagnosing of autism spectrum disorders, but to illustrate ways of handling commonly experienced problems in individuals and families. Parents and caregivers have many similar things to say about how difficult it is for their child to get through most days. Experiences that are usually considered enjoyable are often traumatic for children with autism spectrum disorders. Parents and caregivers are looking for ways to help their children get through the day and to help them enjoy life to the fullest.

Experiences of children with autism spectrum disorders

What is so difficult about raising a child with an autism spectrum disorder is that solely using a traditional approach to parenting often does not work very well. For example, setting rules and expectations alone or expecting a child to learn by watching others is not enough for many children with autism spectrum disorders to be successful in the home and community.

We, as authors, have first-hand experience in this regard. Here is a situation Dion experienced:

> I remember that before our son was diagnosed with Asperger Syndrome, he would come home from kindergarten each day with a note about how poorly he behaved in school. He would lie on the classroom floor, become upset during assemblies, and refuse to follow simple teacher requests.
>
> I also remember getting calls at work from the school principal asking me to talk to my son about his school behavior. This approach did not help change his behavior. My wife and I were frustrated with the school and with our son because we didn't know what to do. Nothing seemed to work.
>
> Shortly thereafter, my son was assessed and diagnosed with Asperger Syndrome. Recommendations included speech therapy, social skills training, and a teacher assistant to work with our son in school. These were fine recommendations, but they were only the beginning of what our son really needed to function effectively at home, in the community, and at school.

What parents and caregivers need to know

Years of working with children with autism spectrum disorders and hours of interviews with parents and caregivers have convinced us and experts in the field that a traditional approach to dealing with behaviors (for example, by using solely rewards and consequences) will not help children with autism spectrum disorders reach their fullest potential. When needed, medication can help support children as part of the learning process. Medication alone cannot give children the skills they need to get through the day. As an example, children with autism spectrum disorders need to learn how to hold an appropriate conversation with a friend. Learning to hold a conversation is an extremely complex task involving all aspects of language knowledge. This requires skills of attending, listening, processing, comprehending, formulating ideas, formulating sounds to respond, and then listening all over again. These skills then need to be applied to different individuals in different settings.

A child with an autism spectrum disorder also requires modifications to the physical environment to allow him or her to make sense of their world. Parents and caregivers benefit from understanding that autism spectrum disorders often affects the child's physiology. Often, he or she does not deliberately choose to misbehave, tantrum, or make inappropriate statements to others. These children are often responding to the physical and social environment with impairments to their communication and social skills and sensory systems.

Parents and caregivers benefit from taking the perspective of the child with an autism spectrum disorder. From this vantage point, individuals can work to modify the external world of a child to meet his or her needs. For example, since children with autism spectrum disorders have difficulty with transitions from one activity to the next, the use of schedules is often needed. Schedules provide important clues for children with autism spectrum disorders to understand their day.

Such a proactive and accommodating approach is similar to adapting public buildings for persons with visual impairments, deafness, or other physical challenges. Children with autism spectrum disorders can benefit by having accommodations made to their environment. These accommodations facilitate access to services and activities enjoyed by children without autism spectrum disorders.

Thinking from the perspective of a person with autism will help the reader understand the recommendations in this book. An autistic perspective includes the knowledge that children with autism spectrum disorders do not understand social cues, such as how to communicate "Goodbye" appropriately. Children with autism spectrum disorders often have a poor understanding of social situations, like how to play with others.

Sometimes children with autism spectrum disorders elicit strong negative responses from other children, such as ignoring. An example of this is one child ignoring a child with an autism spectrum disorder trying to make small talk.

Children with autism spectrum disorders often feel that their senses are under assault. Pervasive anxiety is common among these children. Frequently, expressive and receptive language problems prevent these children from understanding typical speech.

This book is about making reasonable simple changes to routines, expectations, and environments in order to help children feel more comfortable. Helping a child with an autism spectrum disorder feel safe and comfortable will allow him or her to live better. With proper interventions and accommodations, children with autism spectrum disorders will more effectively relate to others and enjoy life better.

How to use this book

Each topic area includes a story about an experience with a child with an autism spectrum disorder. As in life, experiences in these stories are sometimes very positive and at times, very difficult. There is an analysis of the situation after each of these stories under the heading "What happened?" For example, a visit to a shoe store is explained in terms of the reasons why the child with an autism spectrum disorder had a hard time. "Homespun remedies" are then given to help parents and caregivers find solutions to everyday problems in the home and community. Successful approaches to handling these situations come from the authors and from parents and caregivers. Recommendations are given with the specific needs of children with autism spectrum disorders in mind.

1: Home Life

Parents and caregivers know that home life is not typical when you have a child with an autism spectrum disorder. What is taken for granted for most individuals, is often difficult for these children – it is not that these children are trying to act badly or that they do not care about what they do.

The disorder prevents a child from understanding and remembering what we consider simple routines. For example, even going from TV watching to dinnertime can be difficult. It is easy for parents and caregivers to become frustrated. Often this frustration is borne out of the belief that the child "should" be following directions better or that the child is willfully disobeying. Children with autism spectrum disorders are not perfect and can be disobedient just like all other children. Moreover, it is typically not an issue of having the intelligence to do what they are asked. Sensory system, language processing, and other physical issues prevent such children from fitting in easily within the routines of the home and community.

Individuals with typical nervous systems follow signals provided by the environment that children with autism spectrum disorders often do not see or understand. For example, when a parent or caregiver is working in the kitchen to prepare a meal, typically a child will know that the signal will soon be coming that dinner is ready. During this time, the child will prepare him or herself internally for the transition from playtime to dinner. They know they need to wait and to begin to have closure on their play. When the call to dinner that the child has anticipated finally comes, he or she is ready for this transition. Many children with autism spectrum disorders are not able to detect nonverbal environmental signals which indicate a change. For example, they may not associate working in the kitchen with a meal soon to come or getting themselves ready for dinner.

While this chapter does not include every possible difficulty that may be experienced in the home, it does list the most frequently experienced problems as reported by parents. The importance of structuring a child's surroundings is the key to their success in any situation. While rewards and discipline can be used with typical children with a great deal of success, for children with autism spectrum disorders these methods fall short. This is because children with autism spectrum disorders are often responding to internal and external stimuli that are quite overwhelming for them. Again, it is not that they are willfully trying not to follow what they are supposed to do. It is that their surroundings overwhelm them. This is why often the best thing that parents and caregivers can do is to make accommodations to a child's environment.

Babysitters

I was terrified when I first received a telephone call from Mrs. Wilson, Brad's mother, asking me to babysit. I knew Brad and I knew he had autism. I felt a little guilty for being afraid, but I knew very little about autism and I knew even less about Brad. I remembered having seen something on television about autism. In the babysitting course I completed they talked a little about children with special needs. However, that was the extent of my knowledge. I knew who Brad was because we live in a small community and I had seen him around town.

Actually, the last time I saw Brad he was with his father in the grocery store. Brad was having a full-blown temper tantrum because he was not getting a toy that he wanted. He was on the floor screaming in a high pitch sound, crying, and banging his head against his father's legs. I can remember thinking at that time that I did not have the slightest idea of what I would do to handle a child with that kind of a behavior problem.

When Mrs. Wilson called, I knew that she needed a babysitter, because all parents do. I also thought that maybe she needed a babysitter more than most parents because of the demands of having a child with special needs. I asked Mrs. Wilson to tell me about Brad and how she thought I could help.

Brad's autism affected his daily living and I wondered what that might mean for me as his babysitter. She said that Brad didn't speak very much. For this reason, she would give me a schedule and list of things he would need. I felt good about this. She made it sound very simple. I read a little bit about autism, but I found it a little confusing because most of the kids that I was reading about didn't exactly sound like Brad. These children sounded like they were in their own world most of the time and that they would probably need very specialized care. It was hard for me to see how these children could be left with a sixteen-year-old babysitter.

The evening of our first sitting arrived. We agreed that it would be a short evening, not lasting more than two hours. I arrived early to be sure that I had plenty of time to go over Brad's schedule. I wanted to be sure that I understood what I was supposed to do and where I would find what I needed.

The schedule said that Brad would begin the evening with some playtime and then dinner. He would have French fries, a hamburger, and a soda for dinner. I made the French fries and hamburger, but decided to give him water instead of a soda because I was a little afraid that too much sugar in the evening might cause him to become overactive. Everything was fine until I gave him water to drink. Brad flipped out. He shoved the plate of food across the table and screeched. I asked what the matter was, but that only made him get louder. What was wrong? I couldn't figure it out.

I thought that I was doing everything correctly. I had flashbacks of Brad's behavior in the grocery store with his dad. I thought to myself that if Brad's dad couldn't prevent him from having a total meltdown how could I? I called Brad's mom on her cell phone and she said to give Brad soda that was in the refrigerator. I gave him the soda. Brad initially struggled to calm down. He was teary eyed and sighed. I gave him his plate back, and the rest of dinner went fairly well.

Sherry, Brad's babysitter

What happened?

Mrs. Wilson, Brad's mom, did a good job by providing a schedule for the babysitter to follow. She has learned from her own experiences that Brad is a child who requires a great deal of predictability and structure in his life, particularly when there is a major change in routine, as in the case of a new babysitter. Mrs. Wilson and the babysitter, Sherry, were also wise in planning a short two-hour initial session to enhance the likelihood of a successful experience.

It was a good idea that the babysitter came early to get acclimated to the schedule and supplies in the home. However, the babysitter did not understand the reasons that Brad required such a strict regimen. This kept her from understanding that it was in the best interest of the child that she follow the schedule provided to her.

She thought that the evening was going well and that a minor change in the menu would be for the better. After all, Brad is a handsome, "normal" looking kid. At some level, the babysitter most likely thought that schedule was just a guideline rather than an agreement that the child was following and depending upon for predictability. However, the babysitter did not understand the nature of the disability, and, as a result, did not think that she needed to follow such a strict regimen. The babysitter may have even thought that the mother was overprotective when she handed her the schedule.

Homespun remedies

Mrs. Wilson knew that in the past she had experienced the benefit of using schedules with Brad. She understood the underlying benefit to her son after having observed him for many years. She discovered that the missing piece in this scenario was that she needed to take more time training Sherry in understanding the underlying deficits that required the use of schedules with Brad.

The babysitter needed to understand that the schedule was a tool used with Brad that provided him with information about events as they unfold. At this same time, the schedule creates a predictable environment. Increased understanding and predictability reduces stress and leads to better self-regulation. The babysitter also needed to know that because of Brad's significant language delays he did not always know what was going on and could not always predict what was going to happen.

Mrs. Wilson recognized that she needed to describe Brad's disability in greater detail. She especially needed to explain the importance of taking the perspective of an individual with autism. She needed to explain how the disability is in many ways a "hidden" disability. Brad looks like every other child, but thinks and responds differently to his world.

Mrs. Wilson provided a schedule for the babysitter, but did not provide a visual schedule for Brad to view. Such a schedule should be provided for the babysitter. The babysitter can point to each step in the schedule as it comes up. Again, children with autism spectrum disorders need such predictability to help them regulate themselves.

Many parents that we talked to suggest that a schedule for a babysitter is used. A sample schedule for a babysitter may look like this:

Choice playtime:

Use choice board with selection of three preferred activities (Chapter 6 has information regarding developing choice boards).

Eat dinner:

Hamburger, French fries and soda with colored straw (of child's choice).

Clean-up:

- Take plate, cup and utensils to the counter.
- Put napkin in wastebasket.
- Use a soft cloth kitchen towel with warm water to wipe child's mouth and hands.

Choice video:

Use choice board with selection of three preferred video programs.

Bedtime routine:

- Get pajamas.
- Dress in pajamas.
- Potty.
- Brush teeth – review micro schedule on mirror.
- Wash face – review micro schedule on mirror.

Choice settle down:

Use choice board with selection of three preferred settling activities.

Choice bedtime:

Read a short book to him of his choice from the book choice board.

Bees

> It was a beautiful day in the spring. There were two potted plants out-
> side the front door. Walter was three and a half. I said to Walter, "Let's
> go outside." We walked out and there were a couple of bees by the
> bushes.
>
> He flipped his lid, out of his mind, screaming hysterically when
> he saw the bees. After that day, he is scared to go outside or walk in
> the grass because of bees, and today, goes inside when he sees a bee.
> He is now ten. He was never stung by a bee. Somewhere along the
> line, Walter heard that bees could hurt you. Years later when I went to
> an Asperger's support group, 95 percent of the parents said their kids
> were afraid of bees too.
>
> Kris, Walter's mom

What happened?

Children with autism spectrum disorders often think in concrete terms.
This is to help them make sense of the world. Walter heard that bees hurt
people. He took this to mean that bees always hurt people. Seeing a bee
would raise the level of concern in most people. Perhaps they would
walk a few steps away. Children with autism spectrum disorders will
often have an exaggerated response to such a situation and need assistance in learning how to handle possible dangers.

Homespun remedies

While Kris did not have a strategy to help Walter deal with bees, other
parents have recommended several activities to help their children get
over fears. Presenting a mock scenario ahead of time is an effective way
for a child to think about how he or she should act in many situations.
Writing down such situations down is like having a script in which char-
acters can play out different roles. A child can learn very clear communication patterns in this fashion.

There are many different ways of developing such written scenarios.
Behaviorists have used the term "rehearsal" to practice appropriate
behaviors before situations arise. "Social Stories"™ (Gray 2000) is a

particular combination of temperamental traits made adjusting and changing to circumstances of living very difficult and distressing for our son. The behaviors were exacerbated due to his inability to communicate using words. Hadden communicated his frustration and irritability with behavior in the form of crying and tantrums.

We knew about the concept of temperament, but we didn't think that this could possibly explain the severity of Hadden's problems. He really appeared to us to have physical pain and discomfort.

This whole experience brought about huge feelings of inadequacy in each of us because we could not interpret our child's needs. Was he really hurting and in pain? What made things even worse was that we couldn't comfort him.

Brian and Ivy, Hadden's parents

What happened?

Hadden is a child with a sensitive emotional and nervous system, which was evident in his intense responses to heat, cold, and other situations. He struggles to adapt to change and demonstrates a high need for predictability. The medical treatments that appeared to make a difference for a short period appeared to do so by placebo effect for the parents. When the parents began a new treatment, they became hopeful that Hadden's behaviors would improve. This expectation and the change in their behavior towards Hadden may have helped him to adapt a little better for a few days. However, the crying would eventually return to the same level as in the past.

Homespun remedies

Brian and Ivy sought every type of medical intervention before learning that their son's severe agitation and discomfort were more closely linked to his temperament than his physiology. They began to understand that Hadden was a very sensitive baby and that almost every discomfort could be linked to him not being able to regulate his nervous system well. They were then able to enact some effective interventions.

Brian and Ivy began to take a much more structured approach to rearing Hadden. They tried to predict what environments would cause him discomfort. They began planning for those environments. When it was possible to avoid the provoking environment, they would do so.

Once, the family was to go to a swimming meet with their cousin. The pool was known for being a loud, humid, and hot place. Since this environment had the potential to make Hadden uncomfortable, the family decided not to attend. Instead, they met the cousin for ice cream after the meet. Hadden's parents did a nice job assessing the environment and were proactive and positive in making adaptations for Hadden. This resulted in Hadden not having a "meltdown."

Scratching a child's back before he goes to sleep, taking a colicky baby for a ride in a car for calming, and requesting that a very active child "run around the house" before sitting for dinner are ways of helping children regulate themselves. Other calming techniques may include pressure in the way of a light massage.

Telephone skills

Cody started perseverating when the phone rang when he was six years old. He would start flapping, for instance. He seemed to become anxious from it. As he got older, he ignored the ring. We wanted him to learn how to answer the phone. After all, he is able to speak. However, it only upset him when he would listen to the phone.

Eventually, he realized there was another person on the other end of the phone line. We showed him this by using a cell phone to call our home phone while standing in the kitchen. Cody saw that he could talk to another actual person. After this, Cody answered the phone. We told him what to say when answering the phone. He now makes phone calls to family members and at times to friends from school (although we are still working on this part).

John and Chris, Cody's parents

What happened?
Children with autism spectrum disorders have trouble making sense of their world. They feel constantly bombarded by internal and external stimuli, unlike individuals with typical sensory systems.

Making small talk is often difficult for children with autism spectrum disorders. Having to speak on the phone with others who are not present may produce some confusion. In this scenario, the telephone ringing bombarded Cody's auditory system and posed a tremendous social challenge. Even so, Cody's parents wanted him to learn how to use the phone.

Homespun remedies
John and Chris came up with a creative way of solving Cody's problem with answering the phone. It is important to teach a concept, such as talking on the phone, in a simple, but clear manner. Such a method is highly recommended for educating children with autism spectrum disorders.

Getting Cody and many children to talk on the phone is often difficult. Some parents report that they make up "scripts" for their child to use when answering the phone, such as the following:

1.   "Hello, this is the Griffin residence, who would you like to speak to?"

2.   Wait for the person to talk.

3.   "One moment please" or "I need to take a message".

This script can be taped next to the phone and used at any time by the child.

Phones can also be programmed for distinct rings to lessen the auditory stimuli. There are phones with large buttons that can accommodate pictures. Picture cues are very helpful for children with autism spectrum disorders and may come in handy during emergencies if the child has to call for emergency services.

Textures and temperatures

Changes in the seasons have always been a time of excitement for me. I love it when the cold fall weather begins to fill the evenings in up-state New York. It is pleasurable to go from wearing shorts and tank top to those old comfortable worn-out blue jeans and sweatshirt. They are like an old friend filled with comfort and familiarity.

This was not the way Jamie saw it. Changes in the seasons meant discomfort. When Jamie was an infant, most of his clothing was loose-fitting and made of cotton. He was comfortable with this, but when he grew older, I tried dressing him in pants and slacks with a belt, zipper, and snap. He rebelled by taking his pants off right after I would help him put them on. He would then go back to his dresser drawer and try to take out his loose-fitting cotton sweatpants.

As he grew older, he refused to wear anything except the loose-fitting cotton sweatpants. He insisted on wearing them to school, to church, and everywhere else. He would change the pants, but only to other sweatpants. When asked what he didn't like about blue jeans or khaki pants, he would say that they itch or that they hurt. Jamie was also bothered by the tags in his shirts. I would have to cut out the tags in the collar of everyone of his shirts before he would wear them. He said that these also itched or that they hurt.

When special events would take place, the restricted wardrobe was problematic. Our family has been invited to attend several weddings and has declined because Jamie just wouldn't wear appropriate clothing. I would find an occasional sore spot from his rubbing the place where a tag touched his skin.

Patty, Jamie's mom

What happened?

Patty discovered that when Jamie was very young, he was very sensitive to textures of clothing. By the time he was five years old, he would only wear soft, loose-fitting cotton sweatpants and a cotton t-shirt. To Jamie, regular clothing was perceived as painful.

Homespun remedies

For the first six years of Jamie's life, Patty agreed that dressing Jamie in the loose-fitting cotton clothing was the answer for his tactile sensitivities. However, as he grew older, Patty and Larry decided that they needed to aid Jamie in increasing his tolerance for a larger variety of clothing. Patty and Larry began by purchasing soft cotton pants with an elastic waist. This allowed Jamie to wear clothes that looked mature. They then rewarded Jamie for making the effort to try the new pants.

Patty cut the labels out of shirts and pants. She made sure to pre-wash the clothing to remove the sizing that makes new clothes stiff and sometimes feel rough. Patty and Larry also employed a regimen of treatment for tactile sensitivity. This involved brushing his legs with a very soft brush and rubbing lotion on his legs. These activities increase Jamie's awareness of tactile input through his legs and decreased the sensitivity of his legs over time. The next step was to get Jamie to be able to transition from short-sleeve to long-sleeve t-shirts.

Patty bought long-sleeve shirts made of the same material as the short-sleeve t-shirts. Patty and Larry then taught Jamie how to roll up his shirt sleeves in the event that he became hot during the day. Patty and Larry realized that Jamie was not just sensitive to the feel of clothing, but when he had too much clothing on and felt hot, he was not able to find relief. Teaching him to roll his sleeves when hot provided him with control and this increased his ability to regulate his temperature. Over time, Patty and Larry gradually increased the demands on Jamie for tolerating clothing that matched the season and event.

Weather

> I grew up in the state of Iowa in an area also known as Tornado Alley. I moved away to attend college in Toronto, Canada and have not lived in Iowa since. We return to Iowa approximately once each year to visit family and friends. It is a custom of our family to watch the weather reports. Several years ago, we were watching the weather report for parts of Iowa and Kansas. It was a particularly active tornado season that summer. Our daughter Carmen was watching the program with us. She became very interested in the tornados and wanted to know all about them. Before long however, she was coming into our bedroom at night afraid that a tornado would strike our home.
>
> While watching the weather television channel, she learned that tornados accompany strong storms. While we did not usually have a problem with tornados in Toronto, every time it rained, or even became a little cloudy, Carmen would become upset and begin asking questions like, "Is a tornado coming? Where will we go? When will it get here? Are we going to die?" She would ask these questions repeatedly. It was painful to watch her in such discomfort.
>
> Jennifer, Carmen's mom

What happened?

Children with autistic spectrum disorders frequently develop fears that are exaggerated. One of the reasons for this is their trouble with language comprehension and concept formation. The child will hear and process the facts of a story, or concept, but may struggle to comprehend the concept, as in the case of Carmen and tornados. Tornados occur in a specific type of storm, but not in all storms. In this case, Carmen learned the concept of tornados and that they occur during storms. However, she over-generalized this relationship to believe that tornados occur during all storms. Carmen's misunderstanding combined with her weak ability to self-regulate and her tendency to perseverate fueled her fear of storms.

Homespun remedies

Jennifer knew that she had to do something to ease Carmen's fears of severe storms and tornados. After studying the situation, she realized that while Carmen was afraid of tornados, the cause was connected to her difficulty processing the concept. This was related to her autism.

Jennifer decided to use visual materials to teach Carmen through direct instruction. She used visual diagrams to show Carmen that not all storms create tornados. She taught the definition of a tornado, gave the specific defining characteristics, provided positive examples of storms that would spin tornados, and negative examples of storms that would not spin tornados. The direct instruction was used to correct her conceptual error that was acquired because of her language processing problems. Jennifer then gave Carmen a cue to help her remember the lesson. The cue was in the form of a rhyme sung to a made-up tune: "Not all storms! Not all storms! Not all storms! Spin tornados."

Jennifer then used a shortened version of the rhyme, "Not all storms," to redirect Carmen when she began to perseverate on the topic of tornados. Then, Carmen was rewarded with a favorite treat, a big smile, a thumbs-up, and her mom saying, "Good job." As Carmen became less preoccupied with tornados and more responsive to the redirection, her mother reduced the rewards to some special time together.

2: Hygiene

Hygiene is a difficult issue for many parents and caregivers of children with autism spectrum disorders. It is important for a child to be clean and well groomed. This is not only so that such children can "fit in" with others, but for health reasons as well. Children with autism spectrum disorders often have sensory system difficulties that make hygiene activities particularly uncomfortable for them. It is our belief that you will find the suggestions in this chapter save you time and heartache in ensuring good hygiene for your child.

Bath time

> Bathing takes forever in our house because it takes so long to get Hunter into the water. He used to hate taking a bath. I think this is because he couldn't deal with half his body feeling warm (the part in the water) and the other half feeling cold. We take our time with baths with Hunter and he doesn't get upset as much any more.
>
> Jen, Hunter's mom

What happened?

Between water and air temperature differences, the bright lights of the bathroom, undressing and dressing, plus the many activities that take place during bath time, children with autism spectrum disorders not surprisingly find this time to be stressful.

Additionally, many children with autism spectrum disorders enjoy a warm bath or a hot shower but have trouble following the many procedures involved in completing these tasks. For example, a shower requires putting soap on a washcloth or in their hands, rubbing hands together or rubbing their body with the washcloth, and washing all parts of the body. In addition, it requires washing hair using one's fingers to wash the front, sides, and back of the head. For some, bathing or showering is quite difficult to do.

Homespun remedies

Jen decided that it was important that bath time be added to Hunter's daily schedule. She believes that it helps to have Hunter work slowly through bath time procedures. A bath time procedure is posted on the wall and this now helps as well.

Other parents suggest having the child feel the warm bath water with his or her hands before taking off his clothes. A bath time procedure, laminated and posted in the bathroom, has been used successfully by many parents with whom we have worked. The child can see words or pictures to follow while bathing or taking a shower. The procedure (or micro schedule) for a shower may look something like the following:

1. Wet hair.

2. Put shampoo in hair and scrub hair with fingers.

3. Rinse hair.

4. Put soap in hands or washcloth.

5. Wash hands.

6. Wash arms.

7. Wash legs.

8. Wash front of body.

9. Wash back of body.

10. Rinse body.

11. Rinse washcloth and hang it up.

Such a schedule may seem overly simplistic, but for the child with an autism spectrum disorder, such a list can be the difference between a successful independent bath time and having their parents wash their child. Chapter 6 has more information about micro schedules for use during any activity.

Parents and caregivers also have suggested that bath time be done at the same time each night for familiarity. Finally, bath toys are helpful for most children. These methods take away much of the anxiety and uncertainty of the bathing experience. They also help a child to learn to be as independent as possible during bath time.

Brushing teeth

Robbie had trouble brushing his teeth. He used to say that the bristles were too hard and they tickled his gums. But he did like the tooth-paste, not eating it, but just the flavor, particularly bubble gum flavor. We also got him an electric toothbrush. We told Robbie to think about all the plaque on his teeth and just imagine the bristles scraping the plaque off. We asked him to think about this hard. Robbie tried it and it was successful. He told us he started to imagine that his teeth were in a big car wash, brushing and spraying away all the dirt and plaque. One day, he "waxed" his teeth like a car by using a towel after brushing his teeth to "polish" them.

Bonnie and Jim, Robbie's parents

What happened?

Many children with autism spectrum disorders have oral sensitivities in addition to not understanding the purpose of having to brush teeth. The mouth is one of the most sensitive parts of the human body. Nerve receptors are located in the mouth and in the nose.

Gums are often quite sensitive. Poor dental hygiene often leads to inflammation and pain in the gums. While brushing can be uncomfort-able, it is necessary that children have good oral hygiene and brush their teeth. How can they do they do this with minimal discomfort?

Homespun remedies

Bonnie and Jim's methods work for several reasons. The desirable flavor distracts Robbie from the discomfort he felt from brushing. The electric toothbrush allows for more brushing movement in a shorter amount of time (many electric toothbrushes have timers). The story of comparing cleaning teeth to cleaning cars helps give purpose to the brushing activity and helps Robbie to feel like he is accomplishing something. Other suggestions by parents include using toothbrushes with shorter and softer bristles to help reduce discomfort.

Clothes

Kyle had to have all the labels cut out of his shirts. All his clothes have to be cotton. He doesn't like to wear socks. He can't tie his shoes. His shoes have to be very wide so the socks won't bind. Also, when it comes to wearing coats, the wristbands can't be elastic. They have to be loose. He can't snap or button his pants. His pants have to have an elastic waistband. His shirts have to be open enough to let his head through easily. No turtlenecks. His underwear has to be large so it will not bind him. It's hard dressing Kyle.

Susan, Kyle's mom

What happened?

Parents and caregivers have to find the type of clothing and footwear that is comfortable for their child. For children with clothing issues, meltdowns sometimes occur during dressing and undressing. Getting your child ready for school could take half the morning if not done well and with the needs of the child in mind. The clothes need to be easy to put on and take off. Susan's story shows that there are age-appropriate and comfortable clothes available to meet the sensory needs of children with autism spectrum disorders.

Homespun remedies

Susan says that she gets many of her clothes online. It is easier this way to browse, rather than taking her child to the store. The fabric is specified, as is the type of waistband. In addition, sizes do not have to fit perfectly when elastic is used. Susan also says that wider size, slip-on shoes work well.

Some parents who have children with autism spectrum disorders indicate that they have purchased soft gloves that are easy to get on and off. Coats need to have a hood, as many children with autism spectrum disorders may like this rather than wearing a tight fitting hat. Boxers, rather than briefs, may help a child not to feel bound. Pajamas should also be loose and comfortable. Shoes with Velcro, rather than strings, can be helpful and even stylish. One-piece pajamas are not always comfortable for children with autism spectrum disorders.

Grooming

> I am a fourth grade teacher and my son has autism. My son developed body odor about the time he was ten years old. It's interesting because I notice that my students begin to have body odor about the time they enter the fourth grade. I was told that odor is the first sign of puberty. I used to blame parents for not getting their children to wear deodorant, until I became a parent myself. I attempted to get Tyler to wear deodorant and brush his hair. But, for my child, I think the problem was more complicated because of his disability. He doesn't really see a need for brushing his hair, looking nice, or smelling okay. Why do people need to groom? This seems to be his view of things.
>
> Lauren, Tyler's mom

What happened?

The use of deodorant requires the application of products that are often cold and sticky. The fragrance included in the product can be overwhelming. Additionally, brushing hair can feel prickly. Children will not often look in the mirror or slow down enough to do good grooming. Some children with autism spectrum disorders do not consider how they may appear to others. Sometimes, sensory issues, and a lack of the ability to take the perspective of others, result in such a child not being motivated to be well-groomed.

Homespun remedies

Lauren was at a loss regarding what to do for Tyler's grooming. Other parents suggest that it is important to make the grooming experience comfortable for the child. Fragrance-free deodorant may be used to avoid overpowering the child with odors. To make the application of deodorant more comfortable, you may warm up the deodorant by running warm water over the closed container (for gels and bars of deodorant). Spray deodorant is probably a bad idea: it's cold and easily inhaled. Wide, soft natural (boar, goat-hair) bristle hairbrushes are recommended. This helps make hair brushing less prickly.

A daily schedule should include grooming time. Additionally, a micro schedule that includes all grooming activities may be posted in the bathroom. Such a grooming schedule may look like the following:

1. Wash underarms.

2. Apply deodorant.

3. Brush teeth.

4. Comb hair.

The morning micro schedule should reflect your family's grooming routine. Some children are expected to wash more frequently, for example.

Haircuts

My wife and I didn't have the kind of money to bring our children to get haircuts regularly. In fact, when the kids were young, I cut their hair myself. It's easy to do with younger kids when the hair really hasn't grown in. It became time however to bring John to get a real haircut. You know the kind where all the hairs have some semblance of order! We set appointments for our two boys not thinking much of it. Well, John enters the hairdresser's shop and sees these strange chairs with people in them, with all sorts of things in their hair. The smell I think really threw him. It was hard to get him in the hairdresser's chair. He kept jumping out and saying that he wanted to go home.

Talking just seemed to make things worse. I think John had no clue why he was being wrapped in a black cape. I could have joked that he was being turned into a superhero, but I didn't think of it at the time. Anyhow, the hairdresser was quite patient fortunately, and was able to have him sit. She cut quickly. Then she used the electric clippers. The sound and feeling against his neck made him cry. It was several months later that John was diagnosed with Asperger Syndrome and we became educated about his condition.

Looking back, we now understand why John was so distressed by this seemingly innocuous event. We do things differently now. We explained to the hairdresser that John has a disability that makes him extremely sensitive to sounds, smells, and whatever touches him. The hairdresser seemed interested in helping. We picked a time that wasn't busy at the hairdresser's shop so that John could get a lot of attention and there were minimal distractions. The hairdresser thought it best that he not use electric trimmers as he thought the noise could bother John. He didn't wet John's hair either. He also turned the chair towards us, so John couldn't see what was happening in the mirror. Since these changes were put into place, getting John's hair cut has not been an issue.

Frank and Mary, John's parents

What happened?

Frank and Mary's story is quite typical. However, for John, it was a new activity and it was a new place. There were new people. Children with autism spectrum disorders do not do well with change. They need consistent and predictable schedules and settings. This does not mean they cannot do new things or learn new things. It just means you have to take steps in preparing children for these new situations.

John had difficulty understanding what was happening in this new environment and perhaps what was being said to him in the name of helping. A huge part of understanding what is taking place in a new environment is being able to see and interpret nonverbal environmental cues. The nonverbal cues include reading and interpreting the signs, body language, and movement in such surroundings.

John was put in a situation in which many of his senses were bombarded. His mind and body interpreted this as a sensory attack. His body perceived loud activities. He was challenged by the noxious odors from the chemicals and hair spray. People who are hypersensitive to sound and touch may not like electric hair clippers. The sound of the electric motor and the actual clipping of the hairs may be uncomfortable. If not carefully used or if they are not sharp enough, an electric clipper can also pull at the roots of the hair. This is true with plain scissors as well. No doubt the up and down movement of the hairdresser's chair added to John's feeling of disorientation.

The difficulties with new situations, struggles with understanding the environment, and sensory overload resulted in John having a stressful haircutting experience. For the typical child, getting a haircut can be a positive experience. For example, talking with the hairdresser, talking about hairstyles, and watching all that goes on in a hair salon can make such an experience stimulating. For children who have communication and sensory issues and a need for routine, the hair cutting experience can be traumatic. Fortunately, there are strategies that families can use to prepare their children for this daily living event.

Homespun remedies

Frank and Mary were successful in attempting some accommodations for John. Other parents make other suggestions including reducing uncomfortable distractions. For example, ask your hairdresser to turn off the radio. Limiting talking can also help in this regard. It is good to pick a hairdresser whom you trust to tell about your child's needs. It is not always necessary to share diagnostic information about your child. However, if your child is afraid of something, tell your hairdresser about the fear. You can tell your hairdresser that your child has sensitivity to buzzing, loud, and unexpected noises, for instance.

Other suggestions from parents include scheduling a time when no one else is at the hairdresser's salon. Once the appointment is scheduled, begin working with your child in preparing them for the event. Familiarize your child with the routine including who will be there, what will happen, and what you expect the child to do.

You can make a schedule with pictures if needed. This would illustrate the appointment minute-by-minute. It would be good to share this schedule with your child and the hairdresser. Such a schedule can include the following series of activities:

1. Get in car.

2. Arrive at shop.

3. Say "Hello."

4. Sit in waiting chair with book (that you bring).

5. Listen for your name to be called.

6. Sit in hairdresser's chair.

7. Put your arms down when the cape is put on.

8. Watch the hairdresser for her or him to signal "up" or "down."

9. Watch the video that you bring (or listen to the story that your mom reads to you, preferably one with strong special interest).

10. Sit still while your hair is being cut.

11. When the hairdresser says, "Done," allow her or him to brush your cut hair off, and take the cape off.

12. Look in the mirror to see how good you look.

School lunches

I would not believe my story if I had not lived it myself. My son Richard has always had a restricted range of foods that he will eat. He has always liked bread, cheese, and chicken. I can remember when he first tasted pizza. He loved it from the very beginning. He loved it so much that by the time he entered school at age five it was the only food he would eat for lunch. For a period of three years, he would only eat one type of pizza for lunch. I had to go to a certain restaurant each day to get the same pizza for Richard or he would not eat at school at all. After going into the restaurant day after day buying the same single pizza the restaurant manager asked me why I was buying the same pizza every day. I told him it was for my son who has autism. From that day forward the manager gave me his daily pizza free.

Madge, Richard's mom

What happened?

Many of us take for granted the significant number of skills involved in just eating lunch. However, eating is a behavior that involves many different behaviors. It also involves the olfactory, tactile, temperature, and taste senses. In addition, eating includes the sensation of being filled or hungry, the social component of mealtimes, and emotions as well. School cafeterias are challenging places for children with autism spectrum disorders. Cafeterias typically are noisy, have a lot people, and have many smells. Eating is time-limited. Lunch breaks are usually intensively social times and are often the times of the day when general school behaviors are at their worst.

For Madge to have to go to a restaurant every day to meet her child's specific wants was quite demanding of her time. One wonders if she had time to do anything else. Not only did getting a pizza each day affect Madge, but probably reinforced Richard's rigid behavior patterns. How could a parent get himself or herself in such a situation? This is easy to do. Parents want a simple solution to handling complex dietary wants and needs of children with autism spectrum disorders. In Richard's case, getting him pizza each day solved many problems. No longer did Madge have to spend time figuring out what Richard would eat or worry that he was not eating at school.

Madge was appropriately concerned with Richard's need for his daily pizza. Parents and caregivers need to understand that they have lives too. Parents and caregivers need to balance the needs of their children with their own. In Richard's case, he may have benefited from a more balanced approach anyhow. Ultimately, the delivery of his daily pizza was actually detrimental to Richard. Children with autism spectrum disorders often have rigid, ritualistic like patterns of behaviors. The reason they have such patterns of behaviors is that it makes the world more predictable. Simple adaptations to Richard's lunch routine could make Madge's and Richard's life more balanced and realistic.

Homespun remedies

Madge was at a loss regarding what she could do to expand Richard's diet and decrease his dependence on lunchtime pizzas. Many parents say that a good place to begin in helping a child with an autism spectrum disorder handle the lunch period in school is to understand how difficult the setting can be.

The lunch period has to be structured in terms of time, social interactions, food choices, and seating arrangements. In terms of time management the child needs to have a school schedule that includes the lunch period. There needs to be a micro schedule that indicates what happens when in the cafeteria. Chapter 6 has more information about developing schedules for children with autism spectrum disorders. Here is a sample schedule:

1. Get in lunch line.

2. Pick up lunch.

3. Pay for lunch.

4. Sit down at assigned seat.

5. Eat lunch.

6. Talk to your neighbor.

7. Throw trash away.

8. Line up to return to class.

In regard to food choices, parents may choose to send lunches to school or purchase the school lunch. Many parents pack lunches for their children to ensure that there are items that they will eat.

Seating assignments are recommended, as is sitting in a part of the cafeteria with less movement and noise.

School team meetings

I sat there among ten school staff members. There were teachers, a psychologist, various therapists, and an administrator. While I believe that I am well read about my child's disability, I was quite overwhelmed by the meeting. All of the team members were quite polite and helpful. Indeed, they asked for my opinion about almost everything. I liked what they proposed for Jacob for the most part. I disagreed about how much speech therapy he should receive and noted two team members looking at each other. I wonder how I would have felt if I had more in which to disagree. Even though everyone was pleasant, meeting with so many people was intimidating. There was so much riding on that meeting.

My child's development is at stake, I thought, as I sat in the meeting. These people have to get it right. I was worried that I didn't have all the answers and that I had to trust these people with my son's life. I feel that I have to learn everything about autism possible, but I don't know if this is realistic. I feel guilty that I didn't do enough for my son when he was younger and worry that this will affect him in the future. It's all so anxiety producing.

Lucy, Jacob's mom

What happened?

It is difficult to be an objective participant in a meeting involving your own child. While most people working in schools mean well and have a great deal to offer, parents' and caregivers' input at such meetings is essential for developing appropriate educational plans.

Homespun remedies

Even though Lucy has done research and understands her child's disability, facing a large group of individuals to discuss one's child is difficult to do. Additionally, Lucy believes that disagreeing in such a forum is challenging because parents are often outnumbered in school meetings.

Parents are encouraged to learn all they can about educating children with autism spectrum disorders. Read as much as possible about

educating students with autism spectrum disorders. The more information you have, the better prepared you will be for important school
meetings. Parents are often the guiding force in making change for their
child at school. This is not an ideal situation as there are so many
pressures on parents and caregivers for the child just in terms of the home
and community. However, many schools are just beginning to be able to
educate children with autism spectrum disorders effectively. They can
benefit from the assistance of parents and caregivers.

Parents suggest that a friend be brought to school meetings. A friend
can help you to make sense of all of the information presented at team
meetings. You have a right to know who will attend such meetings ahead
of time. Additionally, ask to have a copy of data or reports before the
meeting to have time to review these. These actions help parents and
caregivers understand such information. Parents and caregivers need to
be contributing members of the school team.

One parent said that bringing an expert in autism spectrum disorders
was the key factor in getting the school to make the changes needed.
Staff members seemed to appreciate the information received from the
expert. The school had a tight budget so getting a resource that was free
to the school was very helpful. Sometimes a staff member's resistance to
change is due to not having access to appropriate information, rather
than not wanting to help the child with an autism spectrum disorder.

Support groups are available throughout the world. Additionally,
there are child advocacy organizations that can help parents navigate the
many school and government systems to get support for children with
autism spectrum disorders.

Most parents agree that it is best to remain composed and cooperative when working with school teams. A collaborative approach is
usually the best way to go. Several heads are better than one in making
complex decisions.

Many parents have resorted to legal action to get changes made to
their child's educational program. At times, this is necessary. However,
many parents say that this can create hurt relationships with school staff.
Gentle nudging often works quite well in getting others to see your point
of view.

Sports: Hallie's story

Hallie was going every week to watch her cousin play soccer. She and her mother would follow the team each week. She would sit on the sideline playing with her dolls and flapping. Sometimes she would get up, run around in circles, then sit back down, and flap. Between games, she would kick the ball back and forth with her cousin. She was showing good interaction with her cousin and interest in the sport. However, with her mild cerebral palsy, combined with her autism, I did not believe that she would ever play on a team. I was sad when watching her play with the ball because it reminded me of how her disability was robbing her of so many real-life experiences.

A couple of weeks later I read in my local newspaper that there was a soccer day camp for children with developmental disabilities including autism. I called the number in the paper and we attended the camp. It was a wonderful experience. Hallie developed some basic skills like trapping the ball, dribbling, kicking, and then passing. The camp worked on taking turns, physical fitness, and following directions. Now, after two years, Hallie plays on a special team against other special teams. She is now happy with this experience. And that makes me happy.

Kelsey, Hallie's mom

What happened?

Many parents of children with developmental disabilities and autism spectrum disorders assume that their children cannot participate in many typical childhood organized group activities. At times, family, friends, and community members do not help matters much in this regard. Individuals are beginning to see that with the right fit, children with disabilities can flourish in group sports. It often takes other parents to start such a group and to help a parent see the possibilities for a child with an autism spectrum disorder. Kelsey started such a group and her daughter and other children with similar disabilities continue to reap the benefits.

Homespun remedies

Kelsey provided Hallie with positive sports experiences. Hallie was quite successful. No one knows what a child with an autism spectrum disorder will accomplish in the future. Indeed, one cannot tell which of the young children today will become our best leaders.

It is important, as it is with life, to never give up hope and never give up trying. Parents and caregivers need to think creatively and keep trying new things to help their children with autism spectrum disorders be successful.

Sports: John's story

John has never been drawn to group activities, and for this reason we knew very early that team sports would be out for him. The problem with this is that our entire family is athletic. My husband and I both played organized sports all of our lives. We still exercise daily. My husband bikes and I run. All of our children are involved in team sports and we so wanted John to participate in athletics like the rest of us.

We tried a kids' soccer club when he was five years old. He cooperated by dressing, going to practice, and to games. However, he just stood in the middle of the field and picked the flowers rather than running after the ball like the other children. On one occasion, the ball came in his direction and he actually stepped out of the way so that he would not be caught up in the crowd. This was not the sport for him.

We then tried T-ball and again he was cooperative by dressing and going, but he did not have the physical skills to swing a bat and hit a ball. We wanted to find something that he would like and that he would be able to do. The dilemma was finding the right activity.

Mel and Julia, John's parents

What happened?

John was diagnosed with Asperger Syndrome when he was four years old. He struggles to engage in group activities and would prefer not to make physical contact with others. He does not have good coordination that would allow him to play a competitive sport where others are depending upon his skills to win. The family needed to find a sport that would fit with John's physical and social ability and one that he would enjoy.

Homespun remedies

Mel and Julia needed to examine John's abilities and his interests to find the right sport for him. They decided to begin their search in sports that are more individual than they are team oriented, although a team could be part of the activity. They started with tennis lessons and learned very quickly that while John enjoyed hitting the ball, he did not like running or the heat involved in playing tennis outside. They decided next to try bowling. This was very successful.

The problem for the family was that bowling was an indoor activity and the family really preferred outdoor activities. How could they find a sport that John would like, was outdoors, and included being on a team? Julia thought that swimming just might be the solution. She called the local swim club and decided to enroll John and his sister in swimming lessons. During the first year of swimming lessons, they would often stay after their lesson to watch the swim team practice.

After one year of lessons, John's sister signed up to be on the community pool swim team. John continued swim lessons. After the second year of lessons and observing the swim team, he decided to join the swim team. Julia met with the swim team coaches to explain the nature of John's disability. She agreed to become a parent volunteer for the swim team. John began by swimming one event during each swim meet. Gradually, he became more comfortable with swimming competitively and increased his swimming to three events per meet. This opportunity increased his social opportunities and even allowed him to move at his own pace. He never won a race, but he improved each week. He was awarded participation ribbons for each event and was thrilled with his performance.

Teacher assistants

Jon was dependent on others for all his direction in school. The physician recommended that he have a teacher assistant during the entire school day. The school agreed and said that the assistant would help Jon with his academics and behaviors. The assistant met him to help him get on and off the bus. She sat next to Jon all day long in school.

During breaks, the assistant played with him. She helped him get to the bathroom and assisted during lunch. Virtually every minute of his day was spent with her. We thought this would be a good thing, especially because the school also thought it was a good idea. They even sent the assistant for training. However, I observed him at school a few times. He seemed not to use the skills that he knows, like saying "hi" without being asked. It's almost as if he's now helpless without his assistant. It makes me sad to think that he is less independent now than prior to starting with this assistant. I am questioning whether this is appropriate for him. If not, what do we do?

Jody, Jon's mom

What happened?

Since Jon had a disability with delayed developmental skills, his physician recommended services to help him in school. He recommended special education, special education, and a teacher assistant. The school agreed and began to provide these services.

What many professionals may not always understand is that it is easy to create dependence if too many supports are provided. In this situation, Jody discovered that Jon was becoming too dependent on his assistant and was regressing in his ability to be independent. Many children would not tolerate such interference in their school lives. For children with autism spectrum disorders, the sameness and consistency of the intervention probably relieved quite a bit of anxiety. The child gets used to having to deal with only one person.

Homespun remedies

Jon's mom became appropriately concerned with her son's response to having an assistant with him at all times. Many parents have told us that they needed to question the effectiveness of interventions provided in schools. This is a healthy thing to do.

Based on Jody's concerns, the school made some changes. They chose times during the school day when they knew Jon had success independently prior to have the assistant work with him. They removed the teacher assistant from Jon, and reassigned her to other classroom duties. Jon was given a schedule for each class period to know what to do at each moment. Additionally, a system was set up in which Jon could ask for help when needed. It was the role of the teacher assistant to set up the schedule and other tools to allow him to follow cues in the classroom environment. Individuals without autism respond to such clues in the classroom. By encouraging Jon to use environmental cues, he became far less dependent on a single adult. Finally, this allowed the classroom teacher to provide direction to Jon. It is normal and appropriate for students to respond to teachers' directions.

Therapists

Madison does great with her therapist. I sent her there because she had many social troubles. One time when I was taking Madison and my friend's daughter to football practice, Madison just wouldn't leave her alone. She kept talking and picking on her. The other little girl got agitated and upset. Madison seemed oblivious that an altercation had occurred. The therapist thinks that Madison is doing well because they get along so well. In fact, the therapist wants to discontinue treating her. I suppose this sounds good except that Madison still can't make friends. Madison is good with adults, yet she can't get along with kids her own age. I think that Madison needs to learn skills that can help her make friends. She has to learn how to do it.

Margie, Madison's mom

What happened?

Therapy can help individuals feel better. It can also help them explore their thoughts. In Madison's case, she is already happy. She was referred to the therapist to help her learn to make friends. The therapy sessions did not give her the skills needed to do this, however. Madison needed to improve skills in understanding the thoughts and feelings of others, not necessarily her own thoughts and feelings. Talk therapy to address the development of social skills was a mismatch.

Homespun remedies

Of the parents whose children see a therapist or psychologist, most indicated that the best experiences were with those professionals who were specific in teaching the children how to socialize. Social skills training teaches children how to communicate effectively with others. Social skills training also helps children learn about others' thoughts and feelings. Such training helps children to interpret the verbal and nonverbal communications of other people. Training in social skills is what Madison needed.

Speech therapists and other professionals can provide language skills children with autism spectrum disorders. For example, language therapy would teach conversation skills, taking turns, greetings, tone of voice, and nonverbal communication. These are considered pragmatic language skills.

Valentine's Day

Scott was never big on holidays because it meant that there would be a change in the schedule at school. Usually it meant that there would be some kind of assembly. On Valentine's Day, the teacher would send home a list of students in Scott's class. The kids were supposed to bring a Valentine's Day card for each kid (there were twenty-five kids in Scott's class). Scott would not tell me the kind of cards that he wanted. I would pick the cards hoping that he would like them. The idea was that the kids would write out the names on each of these cards. The problem was that Scott's handwriting is difficult for him to do, so for a few years I was doing Scott's cards for him. Scott became pretty disengaged from the whole process.

Jill, Scott's mom

What happened?

Sometimes adults can be too helpful for a child's good. In this case, the parent wrote out cards for Scott. This created disinterest for him in the activity. Scott may have also felt bad not being able to write out cards like other children. Parents and caregivers need to find ways to help their children help themselves. It is important that all individuals learn skills to help them become more independent. Providing too many supports can hamper this process.

Homespun remedies

After recognizing the problem with taking over writing Valentine's Day cards, Jill decided to use Scott's strengths using the computer. Another parent said that her daughter likes typing on the computer better than writing. Then she prints out greetings, cuts out each greeting, and tapes these to Valentine cards. Another solution is to use a computer program to make such cards. One parent says that she has her son write Valentine's Day cards, two a day, for two weeks before Valentine's Day. By Valentine's Day, her son has all his cards filled out. Each of these methods for completing Valentine cards ensures that the child is fully invested in the process and feels good about participating.

6: Tools for Adapting the Environment for Success

A child's environment poses unique challenges for children with autism spectrum disorders. Many of the homespun remedies in this book involve helping children with autism spectrum disorders to make sense of their environments. These remedies often include how to introduce new settings, experiences, and skills into a child's life. Many of the methods discussed in the various scenarios in previous chapters are detailed in this chapter.

It may be a new concept for parents and caregivers to think that they need to teach their child with an autism spectrum disorder. All parents and caregivers teach, but usually not in a direct fashion, as is the case in classrooms. Parents and caregivers explain and show children how to wash dishes, put away their clothes, and ride a bike. However, children with autism spectrum disorders need more explicit instruction in most areas of daily living because of their unique learning needs.

Teaching skills using the methods indicated in this chapter will reduce feelings of frustration for parents and caregivers. Using these methods will help children learn new skills with minimal frustration. These methods are tools that are used by educators and professionals in the field of autism with tremendous success.

Behavior plans

A good behavior plan is simple to put together. However, it should be noted that while children with autism spectrum disorders can benefit from a behavior plan, more often than not these children respond more positively to making changes to their environment. A behavior plan can supplement environmental adaptations and can consist of the "A-B-Cs."

A - Antecedent

This is the directive given by the parent or caregiver that occurs right before the response from the child. For example, Johnny is told that it is time to get ready for school. Telling Johnny that it is time to get ready for school is the antecedent.

B - Behavior

This is the response from the child that follows the antecedent, also known as the target behavior that you would like to see increased or decreased. For example, Johnny puts on his shirt and pants.

C - Consequence

This is a response from a parent or caregiver that follows the target behavior that helps to increase or decrease this behavior. For example, Johnny is allowed to play his favorite video game for fifteen minutes before school after he gets his clothes on and brushes his teeth.

It is important that the desired behavior be carefully selected before beginning a behavior plan. You need to determine if you want to increase or decrease the specific behavior. If you want to increase or maintain a certain behavior, you will then want to select a powerful reward, or reinforcer, for the "C" or consequence in the A-B-C behavior plan. If, conversely, you want to decrease or eliminate an undesirable behavior, you will want to select a consequence that is undesirable for the child.

Typically, when teaching new skills, focusing on desirable outcomes tends to be more positive and palatable for parents. In the example above, Johnny's parents chose to increase his dressing behavior by presenting a desirable consequence directly after the appropriate response from Johnny.

Choice boards

Choice boards are tools that provide children with choices for desirable activities and rewards. A child can be motivated to complete a required task by seeing the choice board in front of him or her while working. After the task is completed (such as completing homework), the child can remove the object from the board to signify his choice. Items are attached to the board using Velcro.

Rewards can include activities, items, or treats that your child in which your child has a particular liking. You can determine what your child likes by simple observation. Likes and dislikes can also be determined by presenting certain activities, items, or treats to your child and assessing his or her interest. It is suggested that you list the activities and items that your child prefers.

Symbols representing each choice item or activity can then be prepared for the choice board. Symbols can include words, icons, photographs, drawings, or even real objects, depending on the needs of the child. If the child is able to read, the words or description of the activity or item may be used on the choice board. For children who cannot read or have difficulty understanding other types of symbols, an actual item may be used on the choice board. For example, if pretzels are preferred snack items, place an actual pretzel on the choice board (cover with plastic wrap).

You can make a choice board for any time of the day or depending on the specifics of any given situation. For example, you may want to avoid a snack on a choice board if it is used before a meal. This may ruin the child's appetite for the upcoming meal. An activity choice may be more appropriate.

Direct instruction

Direct instruction is a simple, concise, and clear method used to instruct students in any subject area. Direct instruction has been shown by researchers to be effective with students with learning difficulties. Good direct instruction teaches skills in small steps so that the child can eventually learn bigger skills. Direct instruction is a more intensive approach to teaching as it involves a great deal of interaction between the teacher and the student. It is most important that one specific identified skill or concept is focused on during any given lesson. It is important that this skill be observable and measurable.

Here is a sample lesson about learning to use the phone in an emergency:

> Parent: Jon, I want to show you how to use the phone to get an ambulance here if someone is hurt. What are we going to learn now?
>
> Child: To use the phone to call an ambulance.
>
> Parent: That's right! Here is the phone and here is the number you will need to call when someone is hurt (the number is taped

to the phone). The number says, "911." What does the number say?

Child: 911.

Parent: Great! Now let me show you how to dial 911 in an emergency. (The parent models this. The phone is unplugged for practice.) Now you try it.

Child: Okay. (The child dials 911.)

Parent: Great job! Can you practice that again?

Child: Okay. (The child dials 911 again.)

Parent: Now I want to tell you what to say to call for help on the phone. What will I show you?

Child: What to say.

Parent: Great! You say, "Someone is hurt in my house and I need help. My name is Jon Smith and I live at 333 Mercer Lane." (This message is posted next to the phone.) Now Jon, you try it.

Child: Okay. (The child repeats what his parent told him to say.)

Parent: Great! Now let's try it again.

Child: Okay. (The child repeats the emergency message.)

Parent: Great job! Now you know how to call for help when someone is hurt. We will practice this again tomorrow. Since you did such a great job, you can play your video game ten extra minutes now.

As you may see from the example, direct instruction includes some key components, such as modeling the skill for the child, giving the child a chance to demonstrate the skill, and several opportunities for practice. In addition, before the lesson starts, the parent needs to be very clear about the objective of the lesson.

Direct instruction is limited to small steps at a time. For instance, in the example above, the parent taught the child how to call for an ambulance, not the fire or police departments. These other skills can be taught at another time so as not to overwhelm the child. It is important that the child's understanding is checked frequently. Direct instruction focuses on the skill level of the child and what he or she can be reasonably expected to learn in a teaching session.

First-then statement cards

Research conducted by psychologist David Premack (1965) found that people will complete a less desired activity when they know that a preferred activity will follow. This behavioral phenomenon works for adults and children. A first-then statement card is a tool that employs this behavioral principle.

First-then statement cards are typically made from a lightweight material like cardboard or thin plastic. The card is divided into two halves. The left section of the card has the word "First" written at the top. The right half of the card has the word "Then" written at the top.

The required activity is placed in the "First" column. Velcro or tape (a white board may also be used) is used to attach symbols representing each activity. The representation may be in the form of objects, photographs, icons, or words. Initially, a child would only be required to complete a single activity in the "First" column, until the child learns the concept and purpose of the first-then statement card. The child would then select an activity to place in the "Then" column. This provides a visual reminder for the child that they are making progress towards the "Then" reward. It also shows them that they are getting closer to being finished with the less desirable activity, such as completing homework. As the child understands the format of the first-then statement card, the number of required activities may increase.

The first-then statement card needs to be viewed by the adult as an agreement or contract. When the child works hard to complete the first-then agreement, a reward should follow. The adult needs to be sure not to press the child to continue working. This will be tempting to do since the child will improve their work performance using this tool. Remember, the first-then statement card works when both the child and adult hold to the agreement.

Macro and micro schedules

Schedules are extremely useful and important for children with autism spectrum disorders. They reduce the need for spoken language and having to remember verbal directions. This also increases comprehension and improves the child's view of the environment as predictable. Children with autism spectrum disorders deal with internal and external stimuli and need help making sense of what is going on around them. Schedules help the child focus on necessary activities and improve opportunities for learning. For children who cannot read well, a picture schedule works well. For children who can comprehend that words or symbols represent certain concepts, written or icon schedules may be used.

Schedules should not include actual times, but rather, a sequence in order of events. This is because children with autism spectrum disorders often perseverate on facts, like time. The child may focus on the time (e.g., making sure they begin an activity at the exact second), rather than on performing the activity.

Macro schedules

Macro schedules generally address larger segments of the day or week. An example of such a schedule for a day is as follows:

1. Wake up.

2. Put on clothes.

3. Brush teeth.

4. Go downstairs and eat breakfast.

5. Go to the bus stop.

6. Arrive at school, go to classroom.

7. Get on bus to go home.

8. Arrive home and eat a snack.

9. Play outside on the swing set.

10. Do homework.

11. Eat dinner.

12. Watch TV.

13. Take a bath and put on pajamas.

14. Go to bed and read a book with Dad.

15. Lights out.

Micro schedules

A micro schedule is similar to a macro schedule except that it focuses on a specific activity. A micro schedule may also be shown in objects, pictures, icons, or words. The micro schedule allows the parent or caregiver to break down a specific task into small chunks. This helps the child to understand each step of the task.

As with a macro schedule, the micro schedule needs to be posted in places throughout the house that are easy to access. Some parents laminate a micro schedule and permanently place it in the shower stall. Such a shower micro schedule might look like this:

1. Wet hair.

2. Apply shampoo.

3. Use fingers to massage in shampoo.

4. Rinse shampoo.

5. Use bar soap on your hands or washcloth and apply to:

   - face

   - arms

   - legs

   - front

   - back.

6. Rinse self.

7. Rinse washcloth and hang up.

8. Turn off water.

9. Dry self with towel.

Role-playing

Role-playing is a teaching tool that helps individuals learn how to respond in social situations. Children with autism spectrum disorders benefit from such role-playing exercises.

A sample role-playing format is given below. The example illustrates how to teach a child with an autism spectrum disorder to converse with a friend. Your child can take the role of the friend. You would act the part of your child. You will need to give a lot of prompts and hints to your child to role-play new skills.

Roles would then be reversed so that your child could practice the skill that he or she would be expected to perform in real life. It is important that you model and explain to your child the importance of his or her tone and nonverbal communication such as smiling, and how close to stand to someone with whom you are conversing. Usually, friends are excited to see each other and share smiles. Here is an example of a role-playing activity:

Friend: (Smile) Hi.

Mark: (Smile) What do you want to play?

Friend: I have a videogame or we can go outside on the swings. What do you want to do?

Mark: I would like to play a videogame.

Friend: Look at these games, which one would you like to play first.

Mark: Okay, let's play this one.

Friend: That sounds like a lot of fun.

In some instances, as in the case with older children, it may be helpful to videotape the role-playing activity. The videotape may then be viewed by the parent and child for additional practice.

Scripting

Scripts can be used to teach children with autism spectrum disorders to expand their expressive language and social skills. Learning social skills can take place within the context of a script.

Here is a sample script regarding appropriate school bus behaviors:

I want to tell you about a neat kid named Nick. He rides the school bus to school each day. Each day he waits in line at the bus stop. The bus arrives and he gets on the bus. He goes right to his assigned seat. He sits there during the whole ride and never stands up until he gets to school.

Nick sits next to Sarah and talks to her. He talks to her about his favorite things about school. Sometimes he tells her how hard his math class is. When the school bus stops at the school, he waits for the bus driver to say it is time to get off the bus. When the bus driver says this, Nick stands up and walks off the bus.

Sometimes he says "Bye" to the bus driver. He walks to his classroom and gets ready for his school day.

Developing scripts is easy to do and quite beneficial for children with autism spectrum disorders. You can be as creative as you like in putting into words problematic situations that you know your child will face. Parents indicate that it is good to repeat the use of these scripts many times. In this way, the child remembers better what he or she needs to do during difficult times.

Symbol communication systems

Symbol communication systems are used to provide visual cues for children with autism spectrum disorders. Such children have difficulty with the distractions of verbal directions due to deficits in receptive language processing, concept formation, auditory short-term memory, and attention span. Repeated directions presented to these children often leads to their frustration, defiance, and lack of compliance.

Symbol communication systems are a great teaching tool for parents and teachers. It is critical to select the right system for your child's developmental and cognitive level. Symbols can include actual objects, photographs, drawings, and words. Symbol systems include icons. These are standard published illustrations representing language. For example, icons are used in formulating sentences and show all language concepts and vocabulary (Mayer-Johnson 2004).

Parents can use symbols in all aspects of the child's life, for example, in daily schedules, teaching specific tasks, giving choices, prompting verbal language responses, and virtually everywhere that typical language would be used. The use of symbols is not a step backwards for a child. It increases the likelihood that they understand what is expected and increases the chances for success in all areas of living.

Autism often manifests itself as a lack of understanding. Unusual behaviors are often a result of not recognizing what is appropriate for a given situation or even being able to understand how to express themselves. For example, flapping may be viewed as being done because a child exhibiting such behaviors does not understand other ways of regulating his or her body.

Parents are recommended to use any sort of symbol or nonverbal communication as much as possible. Verbal instruction should not be used exclusively, especially when a child is upset, or in new situations.

Most poor behaviors are preventable. The use of nonverbal symbol cues and support are extremely effective with children with autism spectrum disorders to reduce confusion about a situation.

Which symbol communication system do you use? This depends on a child's readiness. Very young children may need objects to represent an activity. Small toys, such as a car, can be used to tell the child that it is time to get in the car.

As children mature, less concrete objects may be used. For example, photographs are effective. Some parents show a photograph of school to tell the child that it is time to get ready for school.

The use of icons would be the next step that can be used as children develop. Some parents and many teachers provide their children with a "book" of such icons. Velcro is used to attach icons to a communication book. The book is usually homemade. This book can carried with the child from home to the community and to school. Additionally, a book can be made for individual activities, like having dinner. For instance, an icon can be available for each part of dinner. The main course icon is replaced by a dessert icon as the child goes through dinner.

When children learn to read, a text-based schedule may be used. Many adults use weekly planners, so why not children? Parents are encouraged to use their creativity in using symbol communication systems to meet the unique needs of their child.

Task analysis

For individuals with autism spectrum disorders, everyday activities can seem quite complicated. Brushing teeth seems like a simple task. However, brushing teeth is comprised of many smaller skills including:

1. Pick up toothbrush.

2. Rinse toothbrush.

3. Apply toothpaste to toothbrush.

4. Make a side-to-side or up-and-down movement against the teeth.

5. Rinse toothbrush.

6. Rinse mouth.

The listing of these sub-skills is considered a task analysis. Tasks can be analyzed and broken down into their smaller compartments. A task analysis is needed usually when an individual has difficulty learning a new skill. Additionally, these sub-skills are targeted in direct instruction.

Parents and caregivers are recommended to analyze tasks that the child needs to do when frustration is observed. By breaking tasks down to smaller parts, and teaching these smaller skills, a child with an autism spectrum disorder, or perhaps any child for that matter, can learn new skills with a minimum of frustration and upset. For example, you may have a child that will get upset if asked to "wash his dish." However, not only may the task not be enjoyable, your child may feel frustrated. He or she may not know how to wash the dish. If you teach him or her the steps in washing the dish and provide visual cues, the chance of a successful experience is much greater.

Wait boxes

Wait boxes are handy tools used for many. It is essentially a select group of items placed in a box, bag, or basket that a child likes to read or use. These items are made available to the child during wait times. There are numerous times in our lives that we need to wait, for example, while riding in a car, waiting in line, and waiting for a baseball game to start. The act of waiting can be difficult for many children with autism spectrum disorders and it is our job to make this time tolerable for them.

Wait boxes can be customized for the child or for the location. For instance, while waiting for a baseball game to start, a small ball can be squeezed and serve as an appropriate fidget. In the car, several books or small cars can be part of a wait box.

Conclusion

The recommendations made in this book can be used in the home, community, and in schools. You are encouraged to share these strategies with appropriate individuals with whom your child works.

It is the authors' strongest belief that we owe it to children with autism spectrum disorders to help them make sense of our world: to make the illogical logical and to make the overwhelming bearable. It is also our belief that children with autism spectrum disorders are gifts. They force others to question why things are so. Why is it that when children fight with each other this is considered normal, while a child with autism spectrum disorder is considered strange for spitting? Why cannot individuals with autism spectrum disorders flap in public, yet a classmate gets away with being rude and bossy? These are the kinds of questions that children with autism spectrum disorders sometimes ask. They are also questions that we need to ask ourselves.

References

American Psychiatric Association (1994) *Diagnostic And Statistical Manual of Mental Disorders* (4th edn). Washington, DC: American Psychiatric Association.

Gray, C. (1994) *Comic Book Conversations*. Arlington, TX: Future Horizons.

Gray, C. (2000) *The New Social Stories Book* (2nd edn). Arlington, TX: Future Horizons.

Mayer-Johnson, LLC (2004) *Writing with Symbols 2000* (Version 2.5) [computer software]. Solana Beach, CA: Mayer-Johnson, LLC.

Premack, D. (1965) "Reinforcement theory." In D. Levine (ed.) *Nebraska Symposium on Motivation*. Lincoln: University of Nebraska Press.

WHEN MYSTICAL CREATURES ATTACK!

✳ WHEN MYSTICAL ✳ CREATURES ATTACK!

1. What is your favorite mystical creature? _____
2. What is the greatest sociopolitical problem of our time? _____
_____

Journaling Prompt: *Write a one-page story in which your favorite mystical creature resolves the greatest sociopolitical problem of our time.*

How the Minotaur Changed the Legal Drinking Age to 16
by Danny Ramirez

He'd be like, "Citizenry of congress, teenagers are going to drink anyway, so you need to learn to trust them, and not have the janitor break open their lockers because you think they have your diary hidden under their gym clothes," which I didn't, Ms. Freedman, so I hope they make you pay for my lock. Then the Minotaur would decree that any teacher who, in the heart of her personal journal, describes students as "feral raccoons devoid of impulse control" is maybe not cut out for education. Then the Minotaur would get hired as a Spokes-Minotaur for King Cobra. He'd be in commercials with all these big blonde Amazonian chicks, drinking forties, doing a topless carwash. In a maze.

How the Unicorn Stabbed Danny Ramirez in the Heart Seven Times, Which Is What He Deserves, for Breaking Up with Me Like That
by Andrea Shylomar

I don't believe in anything mystical, Ms. Freedman. Not even God. You made us build that diorama of Mount Olympus, and you made us paint that mural with unicorns and butcher birds and sand toads. You said it was to show that books transport us to different worlds, where there are different rules, and there's magic in everything. Well what you forgot, Ms. Freedman, is that when you shut the book, you're back in this world, and the bell is ringing, and wadded up paper is thrown at your head, and Phil Gasher is poking at your crotch with a broken pencil, and Kristi Colimote's bitchy flunkies climb into your bathroom stall and threaten you with scissors. What you need is a book that takes you out of this world permanently. Which is called a gun, I think.

How the Werewolf Solved the Problem of Hunger
by Xuang Lee Zhang

He ate everyone. Then there were no more people. Then no one was hungry. Especially not the Werewolf. He did get lonely, though. He was so fat he couldn't move, and he lay on the bank of the river wishing someone would come and sing to him. Nobody did.

How the Giant Squid Made Me Stop Being Pregnant
by Kristi Colimote

I was swimming in my bathing suit, all worried, because like I told you at lunch hour Ms. Freedman, I'm pregnant. I guess Danny Ramirez is the father, but I barely broke up with him, and already he's hooking up behind the dumpster with that fish-lipped Shylomar freak. Plus also? My mom is totally going to kick me out when she finds out.

So I was floating there, and it smelled like seaweed, and I tasted salt on my tongue, and then the giant squid grabbed me with her big pink arm. It felt all squishy around my stomach, and it pulled me under and I couldn't breathe. The squid hugged me close to her body, and told me in squid language that she would take my baby and live with it under the sea. Then she squeezed my stomach and this little fish popped out and I could tell it was going to grow up to be like this gorgeous mermaid who would drive the sailors crazy when they saw her tits all poking out of the water. The squid kind of cradled the little fish with one tentacle and then she let me go. I stuck my head out of the water and I felt my stomach and the baby was gone. I swam back to shore, all happy, because my baby was safe there in the dark water, and in my bathing suit I walked all the way over to the Planned Parenthood on 23rd Street. I was all dripping when I walked inside. The secretaries were like, "What's with this chick?" I just told them to put me on birth control, like I should have done a year ago, if I wasn't so scared of my mom finding out.

How the Sphinx Solved the Problem of Loneliness
by Cody Splunk

As I meandered down the trash-laden streets, a deep voice rose from the gutter grate: "*Down here.*" I looked down there, and was startled to see a basilisk swishing its tail in the darkness. "*Before you dain to pass this gate . . .*" His voice caused tremors in the pavement. "*You must answer me this riddle.*"

"So be it," I said.

The creature spoke in a rumbling whisper. "*Large as a mountain, small as a pea, Endlessly swimming in a waterless sea.*" His eyes burned with the fire of a thousand suns. "*What am I?*"

I bit my thumb, and raised my eyes. The stars were numb smears against the engulfing void.

"You are an asteroid," I said.

The creature threw back its head and gave a roar so great it shattered the windows in a nearby warehouse. Its head spun round like a whirling dervish, and when it ceased spinning, its countenance was transformed.

"You're not a mere basilisk," I exclaimed. "You're a shape-shifting basilisk-sphinx! Never has there been a creature so rare—and so dangerous." I drew in my breath. "According to *Book IV of Engagement with Creatures of Foul Darkness*, you are honor-bound to accept my riddle. So answer me this:

Long-limbed and Learn'd,
I read, game, and snack,
Oh unquenchable longing
What is it I lack?

(See back for answer, Ms. F.)
Answer: Janice Gibbs won't go out with me.

How the Vampire Resolved the Global AIDS Crisis
by Julie Chang

I guess he turned everyone with AIDS into vampires. Then, because they were vampires, they would live forever. And not die of AIDS. But I guess then there would be the problem of all these AIDS vampires spreading disease when they sucked people's blood. So maybe it would be better if the vampire just did AIDS awareness education. He could go around to assemblies in high school cafeterias and tell people about AIDS and show them how to put a condom on a banana, like you did in homeroom after Kristi got pregnant, Ms. Freedman. Except no one would laugh, or ask *what is the difference between an erection and a boner?* or say it didn't look like you'd ever opened a condom wrapper before, because you kept fumbling, and you finally tore it open with your teeth. Everyone would just be really frightened, and use condoms, and not get AIDS.

How the Cephalopod Balanced the National Budget
by Andy Lopez

Cephalopods seem like mystical creatures to me, Ms. Freedman, because they have no vertebrae, and they can change color faster than a chameleon. Also, I was wondering: are those your real eyes, Ms. Freedman? Because there's a lot of light in them, when you stand by the window. I thought maybe you wear contact lenses, and that's where you get those little flecks of green. If the Cephalopods balanced the national budget—I am thinking here of lots of tiny slugs jumping on calculator buttons to do the equations—you wouldn't have to buy us scissors and tape. And you wouldn't be so stressed, because we would have more books than just *Reading is Fun!* from 1972, which as you pointed out, is for fourth graders. You wouldn't have had to bring in all your childhood books from your family's basement, and you wouldn't have been so upset when someone drew boobs and a penis on Black Beauty. I know you think it was me, because of those notes I wrote you, but it wasn't. I wouldn't do something like that, Ms. Freedman. I like you. I think you're the best teacher in the school.

How the Pegasus Created World Peace
by Amelia Basil

I rode the Pegasus to school on Monday morning, and we stood on Ms. Freedman's desk and testified to the rapturous power of the Lord. The Pegasus interpreted scripture and I spoke in tongues. Angelica Masterson fell to her knees and saw a vision of souls tormented in lakes of fire. She abandoned her way of darkness, and no longer made me swallow erasers in second period. Then the seventh seal was opened. The sun turned black, the moon became blood, and stars fell to earth like fruit shaken from trees. The Lamb of God appeared in all his glory, his white robes blinding our eyes. I knelt before him, and he put his hand on my head. "Well done, good and faithful servant," he said. A sword of joy pierced my heart, and I felt the violence of love.

How the Succubus Got Me Laid
by Phil Gasher

I was lying on my bed, staring at these pictures I ripped out of *Playboy* and taped to my ceiling. I wanted it bad. My little brother, who shares my room, was like, "Wanna play Legos?" And even when I looked at the Lego princess, who is tiny and square and yellow, I felt kind of turned on. Suddenly, the room began to shake, and the Lego princess grew a pair of bat wings, and then she grew bigger and bigger until she was this really hot, tall, yellow woman, only with goat hooves and a forked tongue. Due to my comic book wisdom, I recognized her as a succubus, which is a female demon who seduces men and draws away their life force. I was like, Davy, go downstairs, I need to have some personal time with Lego princess.

I lost ninety percent of my life force that afternoon, but it was totally worth it. And that is why, Ms. Freedman, I kept falling asleep in class last week.

How the Wood-Nymph Saved the Environment
by Janice Aurelia Gibbs

It would be kind of like that time that you brought in cupcakes on your birthday, Ms. Freedman, and Andrea Shylomar said they tasted like wet bananas, and you were like, "Very well then, Andrea, give me back the cupcake," and she was like, "No, miss, I was just saying stuff, I'll still eat it." Then Danny Ramirez was all, "This frosting looks like poop." And you lost it, Ms. Freedman. You took his cupcake and smashed it against the chalkboard. The cupcake stuck to the chalkboard for a few seconds, and when it fell off, it left this smear on the chalkboard. Which, Ms. Freedman, you have to admit, did look a lot like poop. Anyway, you just stood there, breathing loudly, and then you made everyone fold their arms on their desk and put their heads down. You turned off the lights, and you sat at your desk, and you ate, like, ten cupcakes. You even ate the wrappers. We were all scared, Ms. Freedman, because you had always been so nice, and you were acting *whacked*.

Anyway, it would be a lot like that with the wood nymph. At first everyone thinks, "We can do whatever to the environment, she won't even do nothing." For a thousand years, the wood nymph forgives us for destroying the world. But when someone cuts down the oldest and tallest redwood tree, her patience snaps. Big-time. She makes the plants wither and the volcanoes explode and freezes the water to ice. Which really makes people think about their behavior. Then maybe they change.

How My Dad Fixed the Lawnmower
by Adam Sandoval

I guess my Dad is kind of like a mystical creature, Ms. Freedman, because he died when I was three. I guess he would be like a ghost now or whatever. Like an angel or a spirit or something. Anyway, I was thinking, what if he came back? My mom would be so happy to see him, she would kick Trent out right away, and say *I never want to see your ugly face round here again, my husband has come back, and he's not going to give me thumbprint bruises on my arms, or lie on the couch all morning putting out cigarettes in cartons of ice cream.* My dad would be a light blue kind of color, filmy and electric. Not just him, but everyone who died and had families missing them—they would all get to come back. Everything that was broken would be fixed, Ms. Freedman, they would even find your journal, which Danny Ramirez hid under the dumpster behind the gym, but don't tell anyone I said that. Everything that was lost would be found.

How the Phoenix Got Ms. Freedman Out of Texas
by Laura Freedman

The phoenix appeared at Ms. Freedman's window.

"You're crushing the gardenias in my windowbox," she said.

The massive bird groomed its wing.

"You may as well come in." She patted her bed. "Have a seat. Can I get you a drink?"

The phoenix shook its head.

"I was planning to have Raisin Bran for dinner," she said, sipping wine from a coffee mug. "But if you're hungry, I'll thaw some chicken."

The phoenix cocked its head to the side.

"Don't look at me like that, bird. I don't need your guilt trip."

The bird widened its eyes.

"I mean, why *should* I stay?" Ms. Freedman gestured with the mug. "Are you going tell me that I'm sowing 'seeds of hope that may take years to sprout'? That I'm reaching them in a way that's 'invisible but real'? Because I've been telling myself that all year, bird. I don't need to hear it from you."

The phoenix regarded her in silence.

"I feel like an empty yogurt container with a banana peel stuffed in it. I mean—can an empty yogurt container with a banana peel stuffed in it transform a child's life? No."

The phoenix fluttered to the windowsill.

"It can't even be recycled."

The phoenix cocked its head to the side. Beckoning.

Ms. Freedman stood up and stepped to the window. She nested her fingers in the phoenix's plumage and hoisted her body onto its back. She burrowed her face in its neck. She could feel its heart reverberate against its downy skin.

The phoenix stepped into the windowbox, crushing a gardenia. Then it thrust out its wings, and flew.

☆ WARM GREETINGS ☆

BRIDGES
Psychiatric Wellness Solutions

Warm Greetings, <u>Laura Freedman!</u>

You are an honored guest here at Bridges: Psychiatric Wellness Solutions. We hope you find that our Wellness Points™ system offers a uniquely effective approach to emotional optimization. Our founder, Dr. Sherman Weir, developed the capitalist model of cognitive behavioral therapy when his son was diagnosed with schizophrenia. Frustrated by the limits of traditional inpatient therapy, Dr. Weir envisioned a system where enlightened self-interest drives positive behavioral change.

How Do I Earn Wellness Points™?

Guests earn Wellness Points™ by participating in activities that activate emotional optimization. Guests can use Wellness Points™ to pay off their Emotional Debt™ and rebuild their Psychiatric Credit Score™.

| Mood Chart | +10 Wellness Points™ |
| Water Aerobics | +10 Wellness Points™ |

Jungian Clay Modeling	+10 Wellness Points™
Journaling Therapy	+10 Wellness Points™
Sand Play	+10 Wellness Points™

What Can I Buy With My Wellness Points™ ?

Macrobiotic Cookie	10 Wellness Points™
Hot Tub Soak	20 Wellness Points™
Letter	25 Wellness Points™
Visitor	100 Wellness Points™

Are There Behaviors I Should I Avoid?

Crying jags	-25 Wellness Points™
Name Calling	-25 Wellness Points™
Passive Aggression	-25 Wellness Points™
Aggressive Aggression	-100 Wellness Points™

(List not exhaustive. Further penalties may be enforced at staff discretion.)

When Do I Get Out?

To obtain an approved release, you must rebuild your Psychiatric Credit Score™. Your recent BIPOLAR BREAK WITH CONSENSUS REALITY has lowered your Psychiatric Credit Score to _0_ .

Can My Wellness Points™ Accrue Interest?

After maintaining emotionally productive behavior for one week, your Wellness Points™ enter the Wellness Portfolio™, where they maintain 5% interest.

Can I Gamble With Wellness Points™?

On Casino night, with staff approval, guests may gamble with Wellness Points™.

Can I trade food for Wellness Points™?

No.

What Now?

By checking in, you've declared Emotional Bankrupcy™. Time to start re-building your Psychiatric Credit Score™! Consult the activity schedule in the lounge for your first Wellness Points™ activity.

Spirit Engaged,
Andrew Schaffer
Outreach Coordinator

✶ THE UN-GAME ✶

Dear Ms. Freedman,

We kept asking Ms. Campos why you abandoned us after break. She said you had "health issues." Phil Gasher says he knocked you up, but barely anyone believes him, especially the part about it being the medical miracle of Siamese twins. I kept bugging Campos until she ripped a kid's drawing off the bulletin board and scribbled your address. *Ms. Laura Freedman, Bridges, 900 Pecan Blvd, Austin, TX.* At first I was like, ah, shit, Ms. Freedman's a druggie! Because a cousin of mine went to a rehab called *Bridges.* On the home page, though, it says, "Guests unwind in the whirlpool, contemplating the exquisite beauty of arid plains." Which sounds like a super-deluxe getaway spa. Then I used my critical reading skills, like we practiced with the toothpaste ads. I realized: you are in the looney bin.

I feel bad, Ms. Freedman. Plenty of teachers have thrown a terrarium out a window and shouted, "You're driving me crazy!" But you're the first who actually followed through. You were so nice to us, too. You gave us extra credit for wearing costumes on Halloween, and you brought in all that cardboard so we could make funny hats. I don't know if you remember, but I made mine a pope's hat. I wore it after school to confirmation class, and even Sister Gloria tried it on.

The substitute we got is not so nice. The Sir. He is really into discipline. The first time Adam Sandoval sassed him, The Sir screamed, "Drop and give me fifty!" We watched while Adam tried. He barely made twenty. We felt bad for him, Ms. Freedman. We pretty much shut up and did our work after that.

While school is not so great, I got promoted at *Elysian Grove*. Kind of. I am "temporary activities coordinator," while the real activities coordinator gets a gastric bypass. Instead of wiping butts, I wheel old people into a room with moldy encyclopedias and tall windows to read "Dear Abby" and the horoscopes. Last week I taught poetry. "The Haiku is an ancient art form," I read from a printout. "It contains three lines, in a syllable pattern of 5-7-5:

> Ancient silent pond
> Suddenly, in jumps young frog!
> Splash! Silence again."

The old people sat there. Carl started eating a crayon. Finally Jean—who is in the rest home at fifty for getting fat and depressed and not taking her meds—scrawled out some lines.

"Jean," I said. "Care to share?"

She scraped back her chair, and read:

> "There once was a maiden from Norway
> With ladyparts wide as a doorway.
> Said her very first lover
> When this was discovered,
> 'I guess then we'll just have a four-way.'"

I did the only thing I could do, Ms. Freedman.

I led them in a round of applause.

After ten minutes of poetry failure, the walkers up and left, and the cripples asked to be wheeled back to their rooms. I looked at the blank papers and broken crayons. So much for my plan of including old people poetry in *El Giraffe*, the Joseph P. Anderson High School Lit Mag. I thought it could add variety. Being the student advisor, Ms. Freedman, you know we get mostly suicide poems. I thought old people might write on different themes, such as tarnished lockets with pictures of dead babies, or gout. I am hoping to God that The Sir doesn't replace you as *Giraffe* advisor. I have such weak-ass arms, Ms. Freedman, and I can only do like two push-ups, so he'll probably fire me as editor and choose someone in JROTC, like Julie Chang.

Anyways, I have still been writing poetry a lot, even though you're not here. I included a poem I just finished. It is called *Eclipse*. I thought maybe if you felt like it you could read it.

Your friend,
Janice Aurelia Gibbs

Dear Janice,

Thank you for sending me your poem, *Eclipse*. I was impressed. Your journaling exercises were always strong, but this poem demonstrates a clarity and awareness that is new and exciting. I especially liked the lines, "Does the darkness hide/ the verses written in your eyes/ the spots upon your soul?" And I was impressed with the narrative turn at the end. "I walked with you for a while/ But soon I found that I / prefer to walk in the light." And nice use of enjambment! You do remember the term? Come to think of it, I'm not sure we made it to enjambment. I think our last literary term was simile. There were no similes in your poem.

You will have to forgive me, Janice. My memory is a bit shaky these days. It's not professional of me to go into this, I know, but I feel I owe you an explanation. In short: there are some pills I take to balance my brain chemistry. In November, I flushed them down the toilet. I had an initial rush of energy—I imagine you recall the lit-term *Jeopardy* board coated with industrial-grade glitter glue (I've been told The Sir burned it in the gravel pit). Soon, though, I felt a strong need to curl in the fetal position in a dark, enclosed space. Towards the end, I hallucinated that a great bird appeared at my window and wrapped me in its downy wings.

My brother tracked me down to Phoenix, Arizona, where I'd been sitting on a park bench, feeding hamburgers to birds. He brought me back to Austin and checked me into *Bridges*. The doctors have gotten my medication straightened out, but I still wake up each morning feeling exsanguinated (look it up).

I want you to know Janice, that, though I had a hard time managing the classroom as a whole, I do care deeply for each of you. It means a great deal that you've taken the time to write. Your nursing home story made me smile. To the orderlies at *Bridges*, I must seem like one of your intractable charges—I refused to attend clay modeling class three times this week. Do keep sending me poetry. I have a lot of time on my hands, here, and I'd rather spend it reading your work than filling out my mood chart.

Fondly,

Ms. F

Dear Ms. Freedman,

I'm glad they got you on the right pills. I looked up exsanguinated and it means, "drained of blood and life." I feel that way a lot of times when I get home from work. Maybe I need some mental meds and a week at *Bridges*, ha ha.

In order to waste time at the rest home on Thursday, I inventoried the supply closet. As I counted crates of tangled string and stacks of brittle magazines, I realized: the "supplies" are just things old people leave behind when they die. Gross. Then I saw the "Un-Game," battered in the corner. I thought: damn, a real supply. An activity for tomorrow!

Me and the Un-Game, we go way back. I first played it at Amelia Basil's house. Amelia's parents believed in exact fairness. They liked the Un-Game, because no one wins. You just take turns pulling question cards like *Who do you trust?* and *Which is your favorite: triangle or dodecahedron?* While I played the game on Amelia's rug, shoveling Cheez-Its in my face, I learned that Mrs. Basil's happiest moment was eating jumbo shrimp dipped in cocktail sauce a week before her wedding.

This seemed sad to me.

Today I wheeled the old people onto the sun porch to play the Un-Game. Aurora leaned down to pick up the lid of the game box. Her eyes wobbled. She put the box on top of her head.

"It's to shade myself," she said.

"Do you want me to get you a hat from your room?"

She held it there, arm shaking. "I have no hat."

"Okay," I said, feeling bad she had Parkinson's, plus also a box on her head. "You can go first." I flipped through the deck, discarding downers (*Share a big letdown in your life. What do you think it's like after you die?*).

"Okay, Aurora. I found one for you!"

It was hard to watch Aurora's emaciated body tremble. It was like watching a grandma be crucified.

"What is your most sentimental possession?"

"My Bible."

"A classic! What's your favorite story?"

"The cripple at the well."

"I like it when Jesus overturns the tables in the temple and drives out money-changers with a whip of braided cords."

Aurora nodded grimly.

I turned to Helen, whose body swelled out of her wheelchair like a rising mound of dough. "Helen. *What advice would you give a young man about to get married?*"

"Buy her . . . flowers," Helen croaked, trying to adjust her thick, terminator-style shades.

"That's sweet. Did your husband buy you flowers?"

"My lover . . . did."

I imagined a lover climbing Helen's mountain of flesh, planting a flag in her perm. "Good for you, Helen. Way to seize the day." I turned to Nancy, a frail woman with skin like dried apples. "Nancy. *What are you most proud of?*"

Nancy brushed an imaginary crumb from her arm.

"Like, what have you done in your life that you feel good about?"

She rubbed her eyes.

"Nancy. C'mon. Participate."

Tears ran down her face. "I'm not proud of anything," she sobbed.

So much for the Un-Game.

Before I worked here, I thought living a long time would automatically make you kindly and wise. Not so much. The old people cheat at bingo and throw hissy fits about toast. Anyways, I'm going to see if I can steal some beer from my aunt, and get wasted, and forget about my day. Don't tell.

Your friend,
Janice

P.S. This is a kind of weird poem I wrote on my break today. It is called, *Nicoli, Who Was Thrown To the Wolves Behind the Sleigh, 1845.*

Dear Janice,

I suppose I don't have to tell you that your prefrontal cortex is not fully formed until the age of twenty-five. Abusing alcohol in the teen years may cause your brain to re-circuit, wiring you for dependence on alcohol or other substances.

But I understand why you'd want to drink. Sometimes the mind whirs and pinwheels, rising and contracting on roller coaster stairs, and you need a little something to blur the flashing lights to shade forests of tree green.

At least postpone your drinking until you make it to college. Please. Alcohol could be your camel's straw—the weight that tips you into the world of perpetual rest home employment. Try that for purgatory.

Sorry I'm jangly. They've augmented meds, seeking that which won't exsanguinate. This new cocktail (of drugs) makes me feel I've swallowed batteries. Energizing yet artificial. I do not recommend.

Naptime!
Ms. F

Dear Janice,

I haven't heard from you in a while, and I worry my last letter offended you. If so: apologies. It's hard for me to tell, sometimes, when I should staple back my tongue. Your choices are your own.

As for your poem. What a strange, lovely opening. "You used to pet the/ soft fur that grew on the tips/ of my ears. Pleasure in the seat of my belly/ as you held me, mother." I wonder if you might consider adding one more verse. As it is, it's a bit difficult to tell exactly what happens after the mother wanders into the snow. Overall though, fine work.

Best,
Ms. F

Dear Ms. Freedman,

Sorry I didn't write. It's just I found out the Smucker's plant is closing down. My dad is being transferred to Piggott, Kentucky, which just happens to be where his jam factory girlfriend (Glenda) was transferred six months ago. According to the brochures, Piggott is famous for hand-carved wooden canoes and Kentucky's only life-size wax museum. I HATE WAX FIGURES! I screamed, throwing a light fixture at my dad. THEY ALWAYS COME TO LIFE AND TRY TO KILL YOU! According to him, that's not the point. According to him, he can't get another job here, unless he works the fields, and his back can't take that. The worst part is, he wants me to stay here, and live with my fat aunt. He says it's because I'm already in school here, but I know it's because Glenda doesn't want me living with them. So now I get to share a room with my cousin Macy, who is always saying things like, "Planning on growing boobs this year, Janice?" Plus, she is pregnant, so I am also going to be sharing my room with a screaming baby. God. I hate my life. Maybe I could come be your roommate at *Bridges*. Ha. Ha ha ha ha. Seriously, though, I'd rather live pretty much anywhere than with my aunt.

Cross My Heart & Hope to Die,
Janice

Dear Friend of Laura Freedman ,

This letter is to inform you that, due to the complexity of this therapeutic juncture, *Bridges Psychiatric Wellness Solutions* has deemed it best to isolate our client from outside stimuli. All mail for Laura Freedman will be returned to sender until further notice. Thank you for your concern.

Spirit Engaged,
Andrew Schaffer
Outreach Coordinator

FROM: janthepiratespy@hotmail.com
TO: lfreedman@anderson.edu
SUBJECT: ?!?

Dear Ms. Freedman,

I am e-mailing you because maybe you will get a chance to sneak away from a nurse and look at your e-mail. They are not giving you my letters because you are apparently on lockdown. God, what did you do, assault an orderly? Jesus. I looked at the *Bridges* website again and I have to say the place creeps me out. First of all, who signs *anything* "Spirit Engaged"? Second, the section on electroshock therapy says "To ameliorate the stress of temporary memory loss, *Bridges* staff eliminates potentially stressful stimuli." Which I am thinking means you are getting electroshock therapy. God. I didn't think they even did that anymore. Does your hair stick out crazy all over the place? I hope you're okay. I really hope you're okay.

Your Friend,
Janice

FROM: janthepiratespy@hotmail.com
TO: lfreedman@anderson.edu
SUBJECT: RE: ?!?

Dear Ms. Freedman,

I guess they are not letting you check your e-mail. Who knows, maybe they don't
even have computers there. Maybe it's "excessive stimuli." Ha ha. Well guess who is
teaching our English class this year? The Sir. Yes. Principal Gutierrez liked the way
he licked us into shape, so she hired him full-time. We are learning lots of literature
under this totalitarian regime, if learning lots of literature means filling out worksheets
while The Sir paces the room, bristling. I have to admit, though, it's kind of cool to see
him shut down the cocky kids. Even Danny looked nervous when The Sir made him
stay during lunch hour for a "conversation." I was lounging on the grass, drawing a
yeti on my jeans, when Danny stumbled out of the classroom. He looked like he'd
been through a wind tunnel.

    "Did he get you with the bullwhip, Danny?"

    "He made me clean out the hamster cages."

    "What does that have to do with you throwing a stapler at Timon?"

    "He accused me of 'inciting irresponsible reproductive activity among rodents.'"

    "*You* put Arnold Shwarzehamster in Tulip's cage?"

    "I wouldn't have done it if I knew that bitch would eat her babies."

    "Dude, you deserved what you got."

    Danny looked me over. "Janice. Way to get boobs this summer."

    I flipped him the bird. I was about to let that punctuate our conversation, but then
I thought, hey. You know what would serve my dad right? If he heard I was hanging
around with losers, such as Danny, who has been in my class since kinder. Back
then he had a head like a T. rex, and he brought his toys crashing down on my head
without reason. My dad hated him.

    "What are you doing right now?"

    "Ditching P. E. and taking you to the lake?"

    "The last time I hung out with you, Danny, you cut the hair off all my troll dolls."

    "Aw, Janice, come on. You're too old to play with dolls, anyway."

    So I went to the lake with Danny. On the way we stopped and got Slurpees and
when we got to the lake we poured rum in them and they were cold and good as
we sat on the hood of his car. When you get to know Danny, it's surprising. Beneath
the cocky asshole exterior, there is a sticky marshmallow interior. We reminisced

about old times, like when Adam Sandoval choked on a golf ball in second grade and the janitor saved him. Danny told me that his dad always wanted him to be a doctor. He worked night shifts at the Discount Mattress Outlet to save for Danny's college, until he had a heart attack while stacking kings. They found him the next morning, hands clutching his heart. Dead.

"You should be a doctor, though, J. You were always smart and stuff. You could be one of those pretty doctors like on TV."

"Not if I keep failing."

"You do good in school."

"Um, The Sir's P. E. class?"

"Smart people suck at sports. It's like, one of those inverse scenarios."

"Wow. It's like you were almost paying attention in math."

"You probably just suck at push-ups because you have brains in your arms instead of muscles." Danny drew a diagram in the mud with a stick. "Actually, your boobs are probably all filled with brains, too." He added two wiggly lumps to his diagram.

"If I have brains in my arms, how am I about to punch in your face?"

"You're the doctor." Danny flicked the stick into the lake. "Don't ask me."

Don't worry, Ms. Freedman. I'm not stupid enough to get knocked up like Kristi Colimote. I just want to hang out with dino-head enough to freak out my dad.

Xo
Janice

✶ BEFORE ✶

BRIDGES
Psychiatric Wellness Solutions

Journaling Therapy I: *The struggle to adjust to a new or stressful environment can lead the emotionally labile to a psychiatric 'break.' Where were you before you came to Bridges? Describe that location in detail.* (10 Wellness Points™)

Name: Laura Freedman

I got used to searing heat hitting my face like bricks from a bread oven. I got used to waking up covered in sweat, nightgown sticking like moist Saran Wrap, used to treating sun-scalded arms with ice and aloe. I got used to pickers on ladders: arms dashing in and out of branches, faces shaded by hats, necks laced with kerchiefs. I got used to the scent of orange blossoms mixing with the smell of hot dirt and moist grass, to round and dripping globes seared open at every meal, to pink-flushed interiors flaunting themselves on our secondhand tabletop.

I got used to the *colonias* bordering the groves: unincorporated regions with faulty electricity, where people lived eight to a trailer or a shack. I got used to walking on the side of the road in the track of a tractor's tread, averting my eyes from dead dogs and smeared cats, watching children bouncing like beans on a trampoline, creaky church speakers splaying salvation—prayers and threats, chants and tambourine songs. I got used to God incarnated on every street corner—used to lugging soiled clothing to Waters-of-Life Laundromat, where tracts delineating the plan of salvation are taped to the top of the dryers, used to buying pink-frosted cookies at De Dios Panaderia—the Bakery of God.

I got used to students who whispered to each other in a language I caught flecks of—students who had crossed the river, or whose parents had crossed the river. I got used to students from Guatemala, El Salvador, Nicaragua, Mexico, Peru. I got used to barbequed corn spread with mayonnaise, squeezed with lime, sprinkled with chili. I got used to kids pooling quarters for cokes, pickles, and paper boats of Flaming Hot Cheetos drizzled with nacho cheese.

I got used to birds: small black birds flying up from behind a building like God had tossed up a handful of currants, birds squalling in the parking lot of the grocery store (drowning the hum of industrial refrigerators), chachalacas—brown robed nuns to the spangled disco dancer peacocks—cackling in the dust of our yard. I got used to the chatters, squeaks, squalls, peeps, calls that sounded like bitter laughter, whistles, flutes, calls that sounded like souls ascending to heaven. I got used to dust and flatness, to sunsets like pink water pouring from the sky, flooding the earth with orange soda. I got used to wind: the hot, cruel wind of afternoon, the merciful magnolia breeze of night.

I got used to it.

But then I had to go.

P.S. Dr. Bin Ladin: I know you have my letters. GIVE. THEM. TO. ME. '

✭ I HAVE BORNE WITNESS ✭

Monica has long curly hair, which always looks wet, and she is wearing a shirt that says: STOP . . . *pretending you don't want me.*

She arches her thinly plucked eyebrows. "Guess who won't stop asking for her cigarette?" She takes her time card from its slot and punches it in the paint-chipped metal machine.

"I'd better go and give it to her," you say, reaching up to tighten your ponytail. But your ponytail isn't there, because you cut off your hair with a pair of baby blue safety scissors last Tuesday, when your car was parked by the creek. At first you thought: I'll stuff it all in an envelope and mail it to Dad, as a joke. But then you looked at the lilies cropping up from the thick ragged vines by the creek and you wanted to go pick them, so you thought: I'll toss it all in the creek, and the water will carry it downstream. So you got out of the car with your hair in handfuls, and it stuck to your arms because of static, and you left the car door open and you slogged through the vines to the creek bank, and then you remembered that instead of rushing brown water, there were just puddles in the creek. So you arranged all of your hair in a puddle, let it float there on the scummy water, and you thought: if some owls dive down and take my cut-up hair for a nest, I'll have done at least one useful thing in my life.

"Janice?" Monica stands in front of your face, drawing you back to the creamy yellow walls of the *Elysian Grove* staff lounge.

"Oh," you say. "Right. Shirley, cigarette." You swing the door open, and burst into the hallway.

The *viejos*, you think to yourself. They will not bring me down.

You discover Shirley sitting on the leather couch by the doorway, next to the nurse's station. "Shirley!" you cry. "My poppet! My princess!" You throw open your arms and stride towards her. Shirley's brain is fried from Alzheimer's. She pops up, propping herself with her rolling rocker.

"Do you have my cigarette?" she asks, animated in her powder-blue leisure suit.

You tear around in a drawer in the nurse's station until you find Shirley's cigarettes and a hot pink lighter. "I *do* have your cigarette," you say. "Let's go outside and *smoke* it."

Shirley wheels her walker onto the sunny, splintery, porch, and sits in a plastic deck chair. You plop down next to her and shake a cigarette out. You hold the lighter while she inhales, widening her eyes cartoonishly. "Thanks babe," she says. Then you light one for yourself.

Jean limps onto the porch in her pink nightgown, plods down into a deck chair, and stares at her feet. All the skin on her body droops and hangs, wads of fat sucked away by a staff-enforced diet. Her jowly face is gray around the corners of her lips. She looks at Shirley, frowning.

"If I ever get like that," she mutters, "Shoot me dead." You look at Shirley, who is staring out at the parking lot like a perky bird. "She doesn't even know who she is." Jean thickens her eyebrows. "It's disgusting."

You remember when the mental home across the street came over for Bingo, wearing seizure helmets, watching you with squinty gentle eyes. Jean got in a fight with one of them. A 'tard called her out on stuffing lucky bingo boards in her sweat pants, dishonorably winning rows of Sara Lee nut brownies. You didn't care, because you had the keys to the prize box. You ate all the brownies you wanted, secretly unwrapping them under the table, covering the crinkle noise by cranking the bingo wheel, sneaking bites between calling out numbers.

"The nuns at my church told us not to kill ourselves," you say, leaning back in the plastic deck chair, crossing your legs.

"Lots of people do," Jean says, widening her eyes, convicted. "When someone wants to, you can't stop them."

"You're a pretty lousy friend if you don't try." You crush your cigarette out in the cement ashtray, smearing black ash into brown sand.

"I was on the boardwalk," Jean says. "In San Diego, when I lived down there. I was walking on the beach at night, and a girl came up to me. She was crying, and she told me that her beau had made her pregnant, and wasn't going to help her out."

"I know the type."

"And she said that her parents would throw her out if she told them." Jean shakes her head. "There wasn't anything she could do. She told me she was going to drown herself."

"And you saved her, Jean. You stopped her," you say, like a calm psychologist. You know how psychologists talk. You have seen the compelling specials on *Lifetime*, television for women.

"I couldn't." Jean winces. She flicks her cigarette and stares at the shadows made by deck chairs. "She just walked into the ocean." Jean stands up. She leans heavily forward on her cane, dingy pink nightgown swinging, and plods off the deck.

Shirley sits up alertly. "Can I have my cigarette?"

"Sorry," you say. "We're out."

"Dammit!" Shirley squawks, pounding her fist on her powder-blue knee. "I want my cigarette!"

"Not now. It's dinnertime."

"Am I cooking?"

"Yes. Everyone's here." I lower my voice. "*And they're hungry.*"

"Shit," Shirley mutters, lifting her walker up slightly and clanging it down on the porch. "Shit." She surveys the deck, conspiring escape.

"Let's go to the store and buy a ham hock."

She raises her head, yellow eyes brightening. "Okay!" She leans up, turning her walker towards the ramp. You jump from your chair and feel for change in the soda machine. You bound over to the doorway, and in. Monica is sitting with her feet up on the desk, phone cradled against her ear, laughing.

"I'm taking Shirley for exercise," you whisper, edging the cigarettes and lighter onto the desk. Then you chase down Shirley, who is on the edge of the nearly empty parking lot when you catch up.

"Shirley-babe. Shirley-my-man."

"Where are we?" she demands, confidentially irritated.

"We're going for a stroll." You lead Shirley out of the parking lot. You walk with her through the neighborhood with gravel streets and plastic toys on yellow grass, corn growing over fences in back yards, screaming kids on trampolines.

"Let's talk about our lives," you say to Shirley, strolling over broken glass. "What's new with you?"

"I don't know," Shirley says, frowning and dismissive, shoving her walker over a weedy sidewalk crack.

"Personally," you say, surveying telephone lines and an armless doll lying on a roof, "Personally I say we go to the park." So you walk Shirley to the park, where an *abuela* in a black and brown flowered dress is sitting on a metal bench. She has the arm-folded resignation of someone in a knitted black shawl in the sun, as she saggily watches her grandkids or her daycare run around the grass. You never met your own *abuela,* your dad's mom. But you inherited skin that browns but doesn't burn and her first name for your middle one: *Aurelia.* Janice *Aurelia* Gibbs, an ugly name-pretty name sandwich. Janice and Gibbs are choppy block sounds, no good for poetry, but *Aurelia* sounds like moving water. At coffee hour after mass, the Mexican ladies laugh that English is good for directing animals, but God prefers speaking Spanish. Ha! No wonder God doesn't answer your prayers.

You leave Shirley's walker outside the short wooden wall of the sandbox, help her step up over its dusty top, holding her thin-skinned hand. You walk across little dunes and mountains to the swing set, turn her around, and push her down in a swing.

"Okay," you say. "Let's swing." You lean back and kick your legs forward, pressing them together. "It's like we're kids again," you say to her, swinging by on a short pendulum of wind, but she is just sitting there gripping the iron links, looking at the sand, surreptitiously skeptical. You swing up, higher, swinging out of this park, out of this town. You are swinging away, swinging some place where things move fast and people talk back to you.

You dig your feet into the sand and rock forward and back, digging trenches as you slow to a stop. Shirley is still staring around the playground, not quite approving. She turns to you, agitated.

"I forgot to pick up the kids," she whispers, face cross-hatched with guilt.

"I picked them up already. I got them."

Then you look at her and think—what if she slips off the swing and breaks her face? You'd have to explain it to Chip, your manager, who has puffy red skin and brings six Dr. Peppers to work each day in an ice cooler.

"C'mon" you say to her, and stand up and pull her up off of the swing, and you walk back across the hills and gulleys of sand, over the wooden wall, across the ratty grass to a metal bench. You sit her down and lie on your back on the bench next to her, squinting your eyes in the sun.

Shirley scans the playground. "Those your kids?"

"No, thank you." You crack back your knuckles. "No kids for me." One more year of high school, then you will leave your home. Be history. Goodbye, Janice. Janice has left the country.

The *abuela* at the next table is giving out purple grapes to her kids. They are scrambling around the aluminum table like vultures or ants, crawling on top of it, then one of them shouts something and they run off for the field. They shouldn't run with grapes in their mouth, they could maybe choke. You know this, you babysat when you were thirteen and keeping it together, putting away dollar bills and dimes in a sock under your pillow.

The *abuela* looks up at you, and you nod, because you are both babysitting here, daydreaming while keeping care of others, lives on hold. She stands up, calling her kids back in, to go home and take naps, or watch TV maybe. She looks at you, and plucks up a bunch of grapes from the watery Saran Wrap.

"*Uvas*?" She dangles them questioningly.

"Sure," you say, reaching out, and she drops the cold dusty blue grapes into your palm. "Thanks."

She smiles at you, showing front teeth framed by metal dental work. Her kids swarm up to her, and they leave the field for some place cool and shady. You hold out a ripe-split grape for Shirley, and as she reaches to take it, you catch sight of a silver charm-chain on her skinny wrist. "That's a pretty bracelet," you say.

Shirley looks down at the chain, and you realize: it is a medical bracelet. Like the kind that warns if someone is allergic to penicillin.

"Oh, this?" she says, dismissive. "I don't know where this came from." Frustrated, she fumbles at it with her thumb and forefinger.

"What does it say?" you ask. You squint down at the line of script carved into the metal.

Engraved are the words, "*Do not resuscitate.*"

Shirley squints. "I can't read it," she mutters.

You pluck a grape, and place it in her palm.

"It just says your name," you say. "It just says, 'Shirley.'"

⭐ THE TURNIP ⭐

BRIDGES
Psychiatric Wellness Solutions

Journaling Therapy II: *Tell us about your father.* (10 Wellness Points™)

Name: <u>Laura Freedman</u>

FUCK YOU, Dr. Bin Ladin.

Stocks

After Vietnam, my father opened an auto body shop, and entertained his ample intelligence playing with stocks. He slipped the family savings into unstable markets, agitating our mother, who wanted the money for curtains, for furniture, for life. Looming destitution unmoored and enraged her. When her emotions riled, he clasped her arms, and shouted, "Pull yourself together, woman!"

A few years after he lost everything in the stock market, she hung herself in the garage.

My brother Steven was eight. I was four.

My father started over, and his portfolio grew. He papered the wall of his office with stock charts, tracking markets with colored tacks and string. He invested in Walmart and Halliburton, and tended his garden of money until it bloomed. Still, he stole toilet paper from the library and ate from dented cans.

Oatmeal

Wearing his navy sweat suit, he stirred gummy oatmeal, fried expired sausage on the stove. In the oatmeal pot went diced apples, raisins, milk, butter, brown sugar. He scraped a spoonful of peanut butter into each of our scratched white plastic bowls, handed us mugs of hot chocolate floating with marshmallows. We stirred as they melted, fizzing, dismembering into froth.

The Poor

At nine, I asked my father if he believed in God. He told me priests in Mexico frighten the poor from using birth control, thus they multiply. He had seen the garbage pickers when he traveled down the coast to walk the beaches and collect seashells. Starving. Half-naked. Living on trash heaps. Better off dead. All the poor should be sterilized, he said.

"And who would get to decide who would be sterilized?"

My father laughed, somewhat stumped. "I would."

"Hitler had the same idea."

"Maybe Hitler was onto something."

Rocks

On trips down the coast, my father gathered rocks. He ran them through his tumbler, subduing their edges, coating them with gloss. He glued a pock-marked, honey colored stone to a copper clasp, threaded it through with a chain, and gave it to me for my eleventh birthday. It was pretty to look at, large and clunky to wear. I nestled it in my jewelry box until the chain grew tangled, the stone unglued.

Pomegranates

My father had a suburban square of flat backyard, crabby with grass, crowded with trees. Plano's heat made branches heavy. The pomegranates were so ripe they split open, revealing red, finger-staining seeds. In college, a burgeoning paper sack of the fruit inhabited a corner of my dorm room, staining the carpet, perpetually threatening mold. Straining for connection, I wrote my father postcards singing its praises as a midnight study snack.

Conversion

Calling from my dorm room, I told my father I was tutoring prison inmates.

"They'll con you," he said.

"A lot of them have really turned their lives around. They've had transformative experiences. Conversions."

"Do you get paid for this?"

"This is the best thing in my life right now."

"People don't change, Laura."

"Not with that attitude," I said, and hung up.

Losing It

"I'm feeling mentally low," my father said, and burst into tears. So Steven drove the five hours to Plano, where he found our sixty-four-year-old father pacing and crying in the driveway. A series of mini-strokes had shorted out his brain, unmoored him in an agitated cavern of dark. My brother took him home, where he buffed his heels with an exfoliating stick until he drew blood.

Walmart

At the hospital, we take turns sitting with him. I am twenty-two. A volunteer program is about to shunt me off to teach school in a dusty border town. I am ready to obliterate the achievement gap, to dismantle the systems of structural oppression and racism that plague our society, to equip leaders of the future with the academic tools to live out their full personhood.

I am liberally brainwashed, according to my father.

Desperately, I try to think of something about my future that will please him.

"Daddy," I say. "I talked to the principal at that school I'm going to work for. And she said the town has the highest-grossing Walmart in the United States."

"I'd like to see that Walmart," he says. A tear runs down his face.

What Is the Lesson Here?

If your main hobby is accumulating money, and your religion is capitalism, the end of your life will be hard. No. The end of life is hard for everyone. Maybe I should say: if your patron saint is Ronald Regan and you reject the weak and the poor, the end of your life will be steeped in sorrow. The end of your life will be unbearable.

Please Note

I'm not trying to get my father to choke down a communion wafer before he dies. That's not important. What I want for him is to experience some kind of opening outward. A healing. A sense of peace. To experience the humming lake of love beneath our feet.

Dostoevsky, Give us Some Hope

In *The Brothers Karamazov*, Dostoevsky tells this story:

A stingy old woman served only herself, save this—she once gave a turnip to a beggar. When she dies, the devils whisk her to the lake of fire, where she cries for mercy to her guardian angel. The intercessory spirit petitions God, who says: take that turnip, see if it will drag her out of hell.

The angel extends the turnip, the old woman grasps hold, and—in a twist of grace—it yanks her from the flames. The old woman cries out in relief. A smoldering soul grabs hold of her ankle, is fished from the lake. Another soul grabs that ankle, and so on, ad infinitum, until a whole chain of souls is flying up to heaven.

"My turnip!" the old woman shouts, when she sees linked souls looping behind her. She kicks. She thrashes.

The turnip breaks. They all fall back to hell.

Mercy Has Crept In

Would a necklace of pockmarked, honey-colored rock pull my father out of hell? A pomegranate? An expired sausage?

I think: yes. All these things would work. I believe that every good thing counts.

The more difficult question: Would my father kick at the wretched souls clasping his ankles?

Probably.

✵ NICOLI, WHO WAS THROWN ✵ TO THE WOLVES, 1874

FROM: janthepiratespy@hotmail.com
TO: vivaloslonghorns956@aol.com
DATE: Thursday, Sept 1, at 3:02PM
SUBJECT: what's up?

Hey Dad,

Just thought I'd send you an e-mail update. I hope things are good at the jam factory. I hear you're working on the low-sugar line. I guess that will let Smucker's tap into the diabetic/overweight market. Maybe you should send Aunt Deb some samples. Ha.

School is going great, except that I have a D in Chemistry. Also, I keep forgetting my uniform and my English/PE teacher The Sir knows not mercy. The good news is I can now do five push-ups in a row. Whoopeee.

Do you remember Danny Ramirez? The kid with the dino head? I've been tutoring him after school. I go over to his house and we shut the door to his room and just study for *hours*. I tried to invite him to dinner. Aunt Deb said, "If he wants to eat with us in front of the TV I don't give a shit." Sometimes (and by sometimes I mean all the time) Deb is in a bad mood. I think she's upset because Macy keeps sneaking out at night to blow truckers behind the overpass. She keeps inviting me to go with, but I'm just like: Excuse me, Danny and I are sitting here on my bed and doing complex math equations, so could you please not open the door at this juncture?

Well, that's all my news! Hope things are great in Kentucky! Give Glenda my love!

XOXO
Janice

FROM: vivaloslonghorns956@aol.com
TO: janthepiratespy@hotmail.com
DATE: Friday, Sept 2, at 8:07PM
SUBJECT: RE: what's up?

J
glenda says kentucky state = good nursing program. think about yr future.
will send jam.
lv dad

FROM: janthepiratespy@hotmail.com
TO: vivaloslonghorns956@aol.com
DATE: Saturday, Sept 3, at 11:09AM
SUBJECT: life/love/oppression

Hey Dad,

I want to be a nurse about as much as I want to be a brontosaurus, and given my grade in chemistry, these are equally realistic career options. I am thinking of going into something more practical instead, like long haul trucking, or poetry.

I am Editor of *El Giraffe* (our lit mag) and this year there's an office space we get to use, with a box where students leave submissions. Unfortunately, the *Giraffe* staff are pretty much the only people in the school interested in poetics, and it's tacky to pick your own verse, and we used to just give them to the *Giraffe* advisor, which was fine when it was Ms. Freedman, but now it is The Sir, who consistently fails to understand my genius. He rejected the following on the basis of "it does not rhyme."

Nicoli, Who Was Thrown to the Wolves Behind the Sleigh, 1845
You used to pet the soft fur
that grew on the tips of my ears.
Pleasure in the seat of my belly
as you held me, mother.

This rock will drink no milk,
you cradle that which crushed his head.
Father, he who drove on, silent.
At dusk you came through the snow,
waving a branch—your eyes were wild.
At moonrise you trace them,
fingerprints I made on plaster.
Mother, you did not see—The sky crackled,
I was swallowed up in light.

I am trying to get The Sir fired. Plan B to get into my own freaking magazine is to sarcastically write dramatic rhyming poems with titles like, "Tears of Blood."

Oh, and dad, Danny and I are going out! Isn't that great! I think it's so sweet. The other night we stayed up till midnight studying. He brought me flowers the next day. The great thing about staying here in Texas and living with Aunt Deb for another year is that I can see Danny all the time!

                        Besos!
                        Janice

FROM: vivaloslonghorns956@aol.com
TO: janthepiratespy@hotmail.com
DATE: Sunday, Sept 4, at 7:05PM
SUBJECT: RE: life/love/oppression

J
you want to come out at xms? see how you like it maybe stay for the rest of the yr. will send jam.
Lv dad

FROM: glendagayle@aol.com
TO: janthepiratespy@hotmail.com
DATE: Sunday, Sept 4, at 11:02PM
SUBJECT: !!!!!!!!!

Listen up you manipulative little shit. Do you think it's good for your father to work a FOURTEEN HOUR SHIFT and then, instead of going to bed with his fiancé (that's right, fiancé, eat it, J) sit awake on the sofa IN THE DARK worrying about his daughter? I happen to love this man. You, on the other hand, are raising his blood pressure with your LIES. I spoke to your aunt Deb and she has seen no sign of any "Danny." She says this "boyfriend" is imaginary. Also: I tried to go out with your dad to O'Shanigan's last night, have some fun, eat some fish sticks, maybe try a $3 margarita, and he spent the whole time worrying about how you USED to be a straight A student and NOW you're doing bad and maybe he made a MISTAKE to have you live with your aunt. Well, little miss, I checked with your school and you are passing all but PE. So. I know what you're up to. You want your dad to send for you. Well. Why don't you just try. You can see if you LIKE living here with me. I have some VERY STERN ideas about disciplining children.

LOVE, GLENDA

FROM: janthepiratespy@hotmail.com
TO: glendagayle@aol.com
DATE: Monday, Sept 5, at 4:02PM
SUBJECT: good one

Dear Glenda,

I can't remember the last time someone called me a hilarious nickname like, "manipulative little shit." You know, if I forwarded your e-mail to my dad, I bet he would find it just as funny as I did. We have very similar senses of humor. Thoughts?

Xo
Janice

TO: janthepiratespy@hotmail.com
FROM: glendagayle@aol.com
DATE: Tuesday, Sept 6, at 11:31PM
SUBJECT: RE: good one

Dear Janice,

Okay. So I went a little overboard. It's just: I love your dad so much. I don't want anything to come between us. I know you're his daughter, but you've always hated me, even though I was better to you than your good-for-nothing mother ever was.

Also: I check his e-mail account for him. He does not even remember his own password half the time. Delete! Delete! Delete!

Speaking of your good-for-nothing mother, she e-mailed him the other day. Found him on the Smuckers website. First contact in nine years. Delete! Delete!

FROM: janthepiratespy@hotmail.com
TO: glendagayle@aol.com
DATE: Wednesday, Sept 7, at 3:58PM
SUBJECT: RE:RE: good one

Glenda,

I am willing to make a deal with the devil, which is you, because it is straight up evil to delete someone's e-mail at will. But if you give me my mom's e-mail address, I promise not to come live in Kentucky. I will stay here in TX with my aunt.

Honest Injun,
Janice

FROM: glendagayle@aol.com
TO: janthepiratespy@hotmail.com
DATE: Wednesday, September 7 at 10:00PM
SUBJECT: RE:RE:RE: good one

Done.

marcia@glitterbobs.com

FROM: janthepiratespy@hotmail.com
TO: marcia@glitterbobs.com
DATE: Thursday, September 8 at 2:03PM
SUBJECT: Hi from Janice Aurelia Gibbs

Dear Mom,

Hi. This is Janice. Your daughter. I am sixteen. I still live in TX, but dad moved to Kentucky as I guess you deducted. I'm staying with Aunt Deb, or as I have dubbed her, "Vortex of Hormonal Rage McGee." I work at a care home to earn money so I can one day go away and be around some people who (unlike Deb) are excited to be alive.

How about you? Dad would get all lockjaw when I asked. I do know from neighbors etc. that you left with Glenda's husband Ray, who left behind a vast collection of commemorative plates. Glenda kept smashing them in our driveway until Dad went outside and told her *stop it already*. Fast forward ten years: they're engaged.

When I was nine, Grandpa wrote and said you'd visited him with a half-sister. A baby girl. Then we didn't really hear from you, which kind of sucked, especially when Grandpa died. He was so nice. I remember when he came to visit after you left. He took us out to lunch at Happy Garden and let me have his fortune cookie. When I knocked my drink on Glenda's lap, he told me I had the spirit of the Comanche warrior.

Anyways, now you know what I know about you, and you can fill in the rest. Also: what is a glitterbob? Is it like some kind of hair product? Do you work in a salon? I'd love to hear back from you as soon as you can write. Deb's place isn't so great. Dad's fiancé has kind of taken him away from me, so it's nice to get you back right now. :)   Okay, well, write me soon!

Xo
Janice

FROM: marcia@glitterbobs.com
TO: janthepiratespy@hotmail.com
DATE: Monday, September 12, at 2:19AM
SUBJECT: Re: Hi from Janice Aurelia Gibbs

Janice Baby,

I can't believe I'm hearing from you after all this time!!!!!!! It lifts me up, honey, like a weight gone from my back. I apologize for not being the best with correspondence. Some of this has to do with your dad telling me he'd break my face with an iron skillet if he ever saw it again. I felt bad, so I tried to step back from his life, Give him space for healing.

I want you to know that I really do love you. Fate just took me on a different path. I could stay in Texas and can jam for all eternity, as your father was content. Or I could be with the man I loved, explore the country and, you know, really *live*. This was the dream. Unfortunately, in Reno, Ray developed a certain relation with cocaine. I was pregnant with your half-sister Casey when he got sent to jail. While incarcerated, he cut out some guy's eye with a chicken bone. I thought it best to sever ties.

After Casey I knew I could never return to Texas. If your dad met Ray's baby he might smother her, like how lions kill each other's babies on the Discovery channel.

Casey is now in sixth grade. She makes good grades. When I look at her I have a pain in my chest because I am seeing her grow up and I did not get to see this with you.

Darling, I am using the computer in the break room, and my shift started twenty minutes ago, so I got to go.

All my Love,
Mom

P.S. Glitterbob's is where I work! (casino)

FROM: glendagayle@aol.com
TO: janthepiratespy@hotmail.com
DATE: Wednesday, September 12, at 9:28PM
SUBJECT: RE:RE:RE: good one

Dear Janice,

I wanted to write you again because I realized I went a little too far. It wasn't right of me to blackmail you into not coming out. It's not that I would mind seeing you. It's just you acted ugly to me. You scratched my eyes out in photographs and poured dish soap on my lemon cake. Once you threw a cat at me! Can you blame me for fearing that if you came out, you'd stop us getting married? But if you promise this is not your intent, I welcome you. (I have talked over this with my prayer group, and they think it fair.)

I also repent I gave you Marcia's e-mail. What you need to comprehend is that your mother is not a person upon whom to rely. Example: She got bored with your dad's quiet way. She got bored with being a mother. She started making eyes at my Ray, and made up some kind of big crazy love story in her head. While I knew by then that my husband was no good, I watched your mother take him away before my eyes. When she left with Ray on his motorcycle, she was laughing and throwing back her hair. I was shoving his things out the window, slamming my head against the wall.

Ray, in case you did not know, was your dad's best friend.

Your father is a good man and I pray that you model your life on him.

Love in Christian Friendship,
Glenda

FROM: janthepiratespy@hotmail.com
TO: marcia@glitterbobs.com
DATE: Thursday, September 13 at 2:05PM
SUBJECT: RE:RE:RE: Hi from Janice Aurelia Gibbs

Dear Mom,

I wonder how well you remember Glenda Gayle. Ray's ex-wife? She apparently is not your biggest fan. But she has always been pretty uptight, so I'm not surprised.

It's really interesting for me to hear the story of your life. It's way more exciting than my life so far.

In youth group this year, Sister Gloria Castillo is doing a cooking and confirmation class. Yesterday we made mini Southwest cornbreads with veggies from the community garden. Mine would have been pretty good, only I forgot the baking soda (sin of omission) and just for the hell of it shook in lots of cloves (sin of commission). Sister Gloria broke a filling biting into a clove. We stood there, watching her root around in her purse for a pain pill. "What should we do?" we asked.

"Discuss suffering," she said. She swallowed the pill dry, coughed, and sat down by the window.

The official story, suffering-wise, is that this lady eats some fruit she's not supposed to. Then God's like: good job ruining the world, you're voted out the garden, oh, and have fun giving birth. Most of us don't think the real God would be like that. Some of the kids think suffering teaches us to be grateful, which I said was bullshit, referring to Exhibit A: nursing home. At the end of the meeting, holding her jaw, Sister Gloria said suffering is a mystery.

It's weird that, after five thousand years of working on this, the official answer is: We don't know. Really. We have no fucking clue.

Anyways, I was thinking I might come out and see you, maybe during Christmas break. I looked up the price of a bus ticket to Reno, and it's not that bad. What do you think?

Love,
Janice

FROM: janthepiratespy@hotmail.com
TO: marcia@glitterbobs.com
DATE: Friday, September 23 at 2:45PM
SUBJECT: RE:RE:RE:RE: Hi from Janice Aurelia Gibbs

Dear Mom,

I haven't heard back from you for a while and I thought maybe I could call you and we could catch up. Then I realized I don't even have your number. You can send it to me, and we'll chat on the phone?

Janice

FROM: janthepiratespy@hotmail.com
TO: marcia@glitterbobs.com
DATE: Wednesday, October 5 at 2:48 PM
SUBJECT: RE:RE:RE:RE:RE: Hi from Janice Aurelia Gibbs

Hey Mom,

Where are you? I am beginning to think Glenda was right about you. Ha ha. Just kidding. Seriously though, maybe you could just let me know you're okay and everything like that.

Also, I thought maybe you could give me Casey's email and we could correspond a little. I'd like to get to know her.

~Janice

FROM: janthepiratespy@hotmail.com
TO: marcia@glitterbobs.com
DATE: Friday, October 28 at 8:32PM
SUBJECT: are you okay?

Mom?

TO: marcia@glitterbobs.com
FROM: janthepiratespy@hotmail.com
DATE: Monday, October 31 at 2:35PM
SUBJECT: my birthday

Today is my birthday. Looks like you forgot. FOR THE ELEVENTH YEAR IN A ROW.

Now I know why dad wanted to keep you away from me.

Don't bother getting back in touch.

✯ TODAY IS MY BIRTHDAY ✯

I sit against my door and I draw my knees to my chest, and I just dial. He gave me his number. It's not like I have the strongest feelings for Danny either way, but I figure, I'm not doing anything, right? And it's too depressing to stay here with my aunt while she sits in front of the television and eats a bag of miniature Butterfingers and ignores the doorbell.

"I don't want to do my job in my own home," she said to me at breakfast this morning. My aunt works in the elementary school lunch line. "You can give out candy if you want to. I don't care."

"Alright," I said. "Maybe I will." And on the way home from work, I stopped in at the Tropicana and bought a bag of candy pumpkins, the kind I like, but then I ate them all walking home in the sun. When the first kid rang the doorbell I sat with my aunt on the couch, watching *The People's Court*, but the kids wouldn't stop with the ringing and the knocker and it got to be too much.

So I decided to call him.

"Hey loser," I say.

"Janice Gibbs," he says.

I scrunch my knees up closer to my chest. "What are you doing?"

"Picking you up."

"Yeah?"

"In ten minutes," Danny says, and hangs up the phone.

I set the shower on the hottest setting, and steam rises from the drain. When I step out, my skin is raw, red, all cooked through. I change into a tank top and my cut-off jeans. It's not like I care what Danny thinks about me, exactly, but I want him to know that I *can* look good.

All Danny's family is there, at his house. In his front yard, they've set up this thing where one of them lies in a fake coffin with his face painted white, pretending to be dead. He keeps a bowl of candy on his stomach. Then when little kids come up to take a piece, he jumps up and scares them. Danny's older cousin is getting it all on videotape. It's kind of lame, actually. Kind of mean, to the kids. Whatever, though. Screw the kids. Kids are brats.

Danny leads me into the den. He hands me a cup of punch, flops down on the orange-flowered couch. "You like action films?"

"I guess." I take a sip of punch. It is strong.

"I got *Lethal Weapon, Die Hard,* and *Die Harder.*"

"How hard can you die already?"

"Or *Barney's Christmas Adventure.*"

"*Lethal Weapon* it is."

So we sit there, sipping punch, watching Mel Gibson shoot people. And we act like it's all casual, but we're sitting leaned back on the cushions, an inch apart. I finish my punch. Then I think, "What the hell!" I finish Danny's punch. Then we are in his bedroom and my clothes are off and it is hot and blurry and damn. Danny knows what he is doing.

Afterwards, we sit there on the couch like nothing happened. Danny's little brother comes in from trick or treating and stands in front of the TV. He's like, two, and he's dressed in a tiger suit, with a cartoon tiger face on his stomach and a hood with little ears.

"Da moon," he says, like it's real urgent. "Da moon."

"He's obsessed with the moon," Danny says.

"Hey, move over, kiddo." I nudge him a little bit with my foot.

"Da moon," he says.

"What does he want?"

"He wants me to take him outside to look at the moon," Danny says.

I sit there with Danny and try to watch the movie but it sort of bugs me to have the kid watching, with all the explosions, people's faces getting tore up, their legs blown apart. The kid's watching it, all serious with his big eyes, hands folded over his fat little stomach.

Danny throws a pillow at him. "Out, Tubbynuts."

I stand up. "I'll take him," I say. "I don't care." I stand and pick up the little kid and lean my hip out so he has a seat. He holds onto my shirt and we walk through the living room, where Danny's cousins are standing around smoking and drinking jungle juice and tossing candy wrappers at each other. I take the kid out into the front yard. The air is thick with cicadas. The trick-or-treaters are gone, and the coffin is empty now.

I walk out into the road, where the asphalt glints in the streetlight, and there are no trees to block the view of the sky.

"Alright," I say. "There it is." The kid looks up at it. I stand there with him, getting cold in my tank top.

The moon is sort of milky gray and the sky is sharp black behind it.

"Today is my birthday," I say.

"Da moon," the kid says. "Da moon. Da moon. Da moon."

✭ FRANKYE ✭

BRIDGES
Psychiatric Wellness Solutions

Journaling Therapy III: *Identify a person in your life who has loved you unconditionally. Describe that person in detail.* (10 Wellness Points™)

Name: <u>Laura Freedman</u>

THIS IS BULLSHIT. I want to make a fucking phone call. Isn't that, like, a human right or something? Also: I haven't checked my e-mail for 6 months! But as I was docked 55 Wellness Points for not going to exercise class (because this apparently constitutes insubordination, rather than, say, a deep and intractable aversion to rhythmic gymnastics) and a phone call costs 30 points in your fucked up economy of mental health, I cannot make a phone call, because I currently have 12 points.

So I guess I'll dig my nails into my thigh and do your exercise.

Frankye

Frankye wore blue sweatpants and gold slipper sandals. Dangling earrings nearly cleaved her earlobes. She ordered dolls from catalogs and decorated her porch with languid, leering ceramic frogs. She lived for visits from the girl next door.

I had fat cheeks and copper hair. Frankye gave me cookies from a red tin. We played with the pull-string doll, the button bucket, the plastic tea set.

Frankye's husband mostly wore a maroon bathrobe, but on special occasions, he wore a suit. Simon was six feet tall and he wore size twelve loafers. He was once a superintendent of schools. Frankye let the milk soak into his bran flakes for five minutes, then brought him breakfast on a wooden television tray. In separate armchairs, they ate before a flashing screen. In separate beds, they played talk radio until Simon snored.

Simon asked me if I believed in Santa Claus.

"Yes," I lied, knowing innocence pleased adults.

When Simon read the paper, he made wild red check marks next to articles of note. Frankye read and re-folded the paper, and Simon walked it over to our house, steadying himself with his cane, bathrobe flapping in the wind. Frankye and Simon sometimes put together a sort of mimeographed newsletter, with *Dear Abby* clippings and cartoons and poems or quotes Frankye hunted and pecked out over at the typewriter.

In the afternoon, Frankye served me soda in a washed out yogurt cup that bobbed with a plastic straw. We watched hummingbirds drain bright liquid from the hanging feeder. When I made straw noises with my soda dregs, Frankye sang: "*You've-got-the-drugstore-blues.*" While Frankye moved damp pajamas from washer to dryer, I studied the *New Yorker* covers papering the garage walls. Frankye also subscribed to *Sassy, Texas Monthly*, and *The National Enquirer*. She sent me home with magazines for my father's girlfriend and cookies for my brother. I slid the cookies under my pillow, and ate them in the darkness. Sweet and lonely guilt.

Frankye went to Betty's Beauty Box to get her hair set. "Doesn't a shower mess up your perm?" I asked.

"I just mostly take a bucket bath."

"What's that?"

"Just wash under your arms and your privates."

I was horrified.

When I was thirteen, Simon fell. At the hospital, his rant concerned a *Dear Abby* column about the need to wash bananas. Rats crawl on the fruit as it's shipped from South America, coating peels with germs. Simon ordered Frankye to make fifty copies of the article and distribute it to neighbors. Then he slipped into a coma, and died.

I read his eulogy. I was not nervous. I liked speaking in public. Afterwards, Simon's relatives filled the house, eating pineapple cake and folded meats.

That night, Frankye changed the sheets on Simon's bed, and I stayed over. I lay awake, listening. Imagining Simon shaking a newspaper over his invaded bed. I strained to place sounds of tapping, creaking. Footsteps. No, I corrected myself. The nighttime settling of a house.

In the morning, Frankye fixed me a tray of black tea and chive cream cheese on toast. I squatted over on the floor reading the comic pages, tray by my feet, blind fingers feeling for the mug.

I slept at Frankye's all that summer. I rang the bell at 7:00 P.M. "Welcome-to-my-parlor-said-the-spider-to-the-fly," Frankye sang. We watched summer marathons of black and white comedies: *Dick Van Dyke, I Love Lucy, The Munsters*. I knit triangular, hole-ridden scarves. Frankye served chocolate chip cookies she had softened by storing with a piece of bread. They were chalky, thick with moisture, crumbly to the touch.

I tried to make conversation during commercials. "What was it like during the depression?"

"I guess it was alright."

"How did you meet Simon?"

"I was a volunteer nurse," Frankye said. "He was having his appendix out."

In July, I felt a pain in my right nipple, a hardened lump unfolding. Cancer, I thought. No, I corrected myself. A growing breast.

"If you're cold, you can come get in my bed," Frankye offered each night. But I didn't. I never did.

At the start of the school year, I slept at my own house. If I didn't have play practice, Frankye rang the doorbell and we went walking. Afterwards, Frankye invited me in for maple walnut tea. One afternoon, she looked up from her recliner and said, "Sometimes I feel like I haven't done much with my life."

"Well." I was sitting cross-legged in Simon's chair. "You make a difference in my life." I turned the hot teacup in my hands. "And you're important to my family. I think that's enough."

I was a smooth-talking fourteen-year-old who did not believe herself. God knew I would not be content with a garden, a doll collection, a quiet neighborhood life. I would make a splash, a *real* difference. Be known by the world.

Frankye liked my blue jeans and navy high tops. We rode the bus to the shopping center, and she bought herself red low tops and elastic-waist blue jeans. The jeans drooped past Frankye's ankles, so she made them high-waters with blue thread. Frankye bought lotto tickets and rubbed the hair of a lucky lotto troll so she would win. If she won, she was going to clear out the ivy and brush in her backyard.

"I think it's nice the way it is." I said. "All wild." I considered myself an environmentalist, and had recently stopped eating meat. At the bottom of the steep-hilled, ivy covered yard, there was a tree fuzzy with peaches. "We should harvest them," I said. Frankye worried I would fall on the hill or be scratched by ivy. I refused to be dissuaded, pulling on Simon's rubber boots, sliding and stumbling down the hill. I came back up with a bag of peaches, small and thick with fuzz. Frankye cut them in half. We swallowed the tart fruit, chewed furry hide.

When I was sixteen I started reading philosophy books I didn't understand: Kierkegaard, Nietzsche, Camus. I stopped believing in God and being nice to people I didn't like.

It bothered me that Frankye would ring the doorbell and ask me to go walking just when I sat down to study. It bothered me when she sang, "You-need-to-get-your-exercise." It bothered me when she stopped on the corner and sucked in her breath and said, "Breathe in that fresh air." It bothered me when she reached for my hand. I took to folding my arms across my chest as soon as I stepped out the door.

Frankye thought of me as her best friend.

I thought of myself as perceptive. I saw through to the lies wound up in small, sad, lives.

Frankye gave me clothes she bought forty years ago, in New York City. I hung the strange and dated dresses in the back of my closet.

Frankye invited me over to watch the *Teen Choice Awards* on VH1. While we watched, I wrote an acerbic cultural critique in my head. During the commercial, Frankye made maple walnut tea. When the show ended, Frankye said, "You don't seem much like one of those teenagers."

"Thank you," I said.

"Do you want to watch *Touch of an Angel*?"

"I have to study for Bio."

"Do you want to go for a walk?"

"I have to work on my college applications."

"Do you want to stay all night?"

"I have finals."

Something inside me was tearing apart. When I became very still, the light went out of things.

I held Frankye's hand when we went walking because Frankye had become wobbly. She needed my hand for support. Purple veins showed through paper-thin skin. We sat down on the sidewalk to rest.

I went inside with Frankye and brought her water in a yogurt cup.

"If anything happens," Frankye said. "There's something for you inside the clock."

"Nothing's going to happen," I said. "You'll be fine."

I got a note in my desk the next day, taped there by the lady in the office. Frankye was dead.

I reached into the belly of the clock, and pulled out handful after handful of cash. Stacks of tens and twenties wrapped in rubber bands. Money set aside from social security. Five thousand dollars in all.

I went home and sat in the yellow bathtub, sobbing.

For Frankye, there was a small gathering in a neighbor's living room. No cake. A lawyer sorted through her things. Frankye left me her dolls. I asked if I could also have the button bucket. The lawyer said, "of course."

I was accepted by every college I'd applied to. The news did not move me. Something inside me had shut down. Food tasted like sawdust. I wanted to die.

After my high school graduation party, I wrote apology notes. I made a noose from an orange electrical cord in the garage. I put my wrist in it, let it tighten.

I stood there.

I took the cordless phone outside, and called a friend.

In college, I started being kind to people I did not like. Including myself. I started believing in God again. I got through my life.

At home for Christmas, I found Frankye's coats and dresses in the garage. I took them back to college, and wore them around.

"Nice dress," a teaching assistant said. "Is that pulled wool? Vintage? Where did you get that?"

"It belonged to my neighbor," I said. "It belonged to my best friend."

✴ RECIPES FOR DISASTER ✴

A fundraising cookbook assembled by the Methodist Women of Piggot, Kentucky

Sweet and Sour Party Meatballs
by Glenda Gayle, Treasurer

Ingredients: 1 package ground beef, 1 32-oz jar grape jelly, ⅓ cup Worcestershire sauce, ⅓ cup vinegar, ⅓ cup flour, 1 tsp oregano, 1 tsp thyme.

Directions: This dish can mark an occasion that is both sour and sweet, such as when my fiancé's daughter came up for our wedding. In a way, it was sweet, because just as raw beef is reconciled with sauce and spices when rolled into balls, the visit marked reconciliation: Janice volunteered to help with preparations for our Biblical Days wedding (with the youth group hired to play famous figures of the New Testament, Bible-era robes for guests, a harpist dressed as King David, and palm leaves affixed to the ceiling of the fellowship hall). And just as the meatballs are doused in vinegar, this is what I felt in my throat on witnessing Janice's new "look": jeans splattered with red paint, sliced and re-fastened by straps and chains, a homemade hack job of her beautiful black hair, and a tee shirt reading "Evil Keeps Me Young." But as Effie said at meeting last week: when you're a stepparent, you kill with kindness. There's nothing to do but take out your nicest plate, stick fancy party toothpicks in the meatballs, and say "welcome home."

Broccomole Dip
by Edna Wertheimer

Ingredients: You guessed it! Instead of avocados, this guacamole-like dip uses broccoli and mayonnaise to create a dip that is just as green as guac, but lower in fat.

Directions: In a food processor, chop up five pounds of steamed broccoli, then mash it with Miracle Whip. As you blend the rubbery white mayonnaise with the fibrous broccoli, think about how you are fulfilling a craving for decadent and destructive guacamole for something which is less tasty. But cheap. It's like the time I developed a problem with the online slot machine. But the Lord conquered that addiction, by, when the gambling bug nibbled at my intestines, telling me: *Edna, you just go right down to the Laundromat and you put a fiver in that change machine.* Then all those quarters came clinking out, and it was like winning the jackpot without having to suffer fifteen thousand in credit card debt and a lien on my home. Of course, the Laundromat is unfortunately also where Satan tempted me into the arms of Enrico the floor waxer. And now whenever my husband sees a quarter, he has an overwhelming urge to smash a piece of furniture.

But Pastor Owens gave us some very good counseling, suggesting we plunk those quarters into the parking meters of strangers whom we do not know, so that when Jesus is dividing up lambs from goats he will say, "Verily, verily, I say unto thee: when thou fed the meter of the least of these, thou fed it unto me."

Valley of the Shadow of Death by Chocolate Cake
by Frances Trigg

Ingredients: Boxed chocolate cake mix, 1 stick butter, 2 eggs, 1 tsp vanilla extract, ½ cup instant coffee crystals, 2 bags chocolate chips, 1 jar hot fudge sauce.

Directions: As the cake rises, call the kids around, and tell them about your girlhood, when you had polio, and Dad made you a special sleigh to ride behind the donkey during plowing season, so you could mash manure into the ground with a stick. We never had luxuries such as Death by Chocolate Cake! During the winter of '38, we were so hungry we ate the seed corn. Then we ate the milk-cow. Then we ate Andrew. Andrew was our dog. Ask the children if they know where Hush Puppies come from. Then give them their dessert.

Dark Night of the Soul Food
by Pastor Theodore Owens

Ingredients: 1 pound cubed stew beef, ½ cup celery, ½ cup okra, ½ cup sliced onions, ½ cup green peppers, 1 large can tomato sauce, rice, chili powder, oregano, thyme.

Directions: Sauté vegetables until soft. Add spices, tomato sauce, and meat. As you stir, cut pages from your youthful diary into snowflakes, wondering just when you lost your faith in man's capacity to turn from his history of violence and build a new earth. Open the newspaper and confront the mystery of suffering: our children killing children in desolate landscapes, faces and heartbeats defined as collateral damage, a local parent who beat his toddler with a board. Realize that you don't know Jesus, that you have never known him, and feel a spreading flush of sorrow at the infinite mystery of the other. *Serve with cornbread.*

The Lord Is My Shepherd Shepherd's Pie
by Darla Green

Ingredients: Instant Mashed Potatoes, Milk, Butter, Ground Beef, Onions, Carrots, Peas.

Directions: Take some powdered mashed potatoes; mash with milk and butter. While the beef browns, imagine King David (who was a shepherd boy before he was a king) chowing down on this pie out in a field, encircled by sheep. Perhaps he would think, in that context, *since I am eating this delicious Shepherd's pie—truly this shows me the Lord really is my shepherd.* Think of how Jesus has been your shepherd always, herding you into church, Bible college, marriage, watching over you when your husband came home drunk and hit you with a broomstick. If you wandered away from the pen, you would fall into a ravine, or be eaten by wolves, so you stayed, doing what the others did, eating, waiting. Find yourself shouting, "I am not a sheep! I am a person, and I have feelings!" When your husband walks in and asks why the racket, tell him you burned the peas.

Render unto Cesar Salad
by Effie McGowan, Church Secretary

Ingredients: 3 cups diced romaine lettuce, 1 can anchovies, 1 cup diced tomatoes, 1 cup shredded parmesan, 1 jar Cesar salad dressing.

Directions: Dicing anchovies is a wholesome anger outlet for when you hear parishioners talking about Pastor Owens behind his back, saying, "The last time I brought him a quart of stew, he was sitting at the kitchen table, unraveling a mix tape, his fingers all tangled with its glossy insides." Or: "His phone was in his crisper." Or "I told him I couldn't decide between a red or black SUV and he looked up from his tea and said, "What would Jesus buy?" Then he mentioned that the County AIDS Hospice was shutting down from lack of funds. Yes, Pastor Owens may be growing a little snappy in his old age, but as he has humbly served this community for over 25 years, perhaps we could find it within our hearts to offer him some shred of grace.

Drinking Alone Cherry Soda
by Neva Patterson

Ingredients: A tumbler, bourbon, maraschino cherries, grenadine, Sprite.

Directions: Put your husband down for a nap, turn on the television, and tell the hospice worker you're drinking strawberry Metamucil. This county may be dry, but everyone needs a little comfort, whether it comes from the souls of other humans or bourbon. It's like the time Darla Green was chosen to play Mary in the Christmas play, and she had just lost a baby, and when it came time to put the plastic doll back down in the manger, she couldn't do it. She just kept holding onto it and rocking. This was Christmas Eve, the holiest night of the year, with the whole church watching. We all sat there, in absolute silence. We knew she just needed a little more time.

Smothered Chicken Casserole
by Janice Gibbs

Ingredients: 6 chicken breasts, cooked pasta, Cream of mushroom soup.

Directions: Follow directions on can. As you set a plate before your stepmom-to-be, say, "Gosh, I just don't know where I got the inspiration to make SMOTHERED chicken casserole. It has NOTHING to do with the fact you spent the last eight hours making me look at fabric swatches. NOTHING WHATSOEVER." Watch her chew, swallow, breathe, and say, "I didn't know you could cook, Janice. This tastes lovely." Reply that you do not even consider this cooking.

Keeping It Together Easter Bunny Cake
by Minny Sherman

Ingredients: Two round cakes, white frosting, shredded coconut, black licorice, jellybeans.

Preparation: Put the babies in the crib, it's okay if they cry, crying won't kill them. It might kill you, though. You know this. Still: you are making a cake, a cake for the Sunday School Cakewalk, a bunny-shaped cake, with coconut fur and jellybean eyes that hide a darkness no man can know. The bunny sees what God cannot. The bunny sees where your heart is, how it wants to stop. But it can't, bunny. It can't. You pat the bunny, getting coconut fur on your hands, letting the babies lick your fingers, until Francis Trig rings the doorbell, takes the babies, and pushes you outside.

Stand in the garden. Feel sunlight on your arms.

Lamb of God Chops
by Pastor Theodore Owens

Ingredients: A meat mallet, 2 lamb chops, ½ cup flour, ½ tsp cayenne pepper, 1 tsp salt, ½ cup oil.

Directions: Synchronize the mallet to the beating of your heart, pounding chops till tender. Remember when your 14-year-old grandson, a sweet boy who died in a house fire, said he distrusted "organized religion." Ask yourself if, in your longing for clarity and order, you have negated contradiction and paradox. Perhaps your old witness is broken. Perhaps you need *disorganized religion*. As realization penetrates your heart like a vibrating gong, coat chops in flour mixture. Fry three minutes on each side. *Garnish with rosemary.*

Walking on Watercress Sandwiches
by Janice Gibbs

Ingredients: 12 pieces sliced white bread, 1 cup cream cheese, 1 cup watercress.

Directions: As you spread bread slices with cream cheese, tune out the cackle-laughter carbonating the living room, where Glenda and your dad are drinking champagne and scrawling toasts on napkins. Slice sandwiches into triangles, sipping from your own bottle under the sink, gritting your teeth. As you cut away crusts, notice a soft loping chuckle. Your father's laughter—a happy, animal, sound. Burn your throat with liquid courage. Sputter and cough. Resolve to wear the stupid robe, clap for the couple, leap for the goddamn bouquet.

Feeding the Multitude
by Pastor Theodore Owens

Ingredients: A church-hall Biblical Days wedding reception, a full buffet, wedding cake.

Directions: In an act of religious disorganization, forget to cancel the homeless dinner. Watch as the ragged throng invades the ranks of the pious. While homeless help themselves to handfuls of buffet shrimp, the churchgoers cough nervous coughs of righteousness. They know—Jesus watches them from the eyes of the poor. And Jesus has walked in on them while they were eating cake without him. There is nothing to do but make it up to Jesus, by inviting him to sit at their tables, share in their food. And it is as on the hill of Galilee, when he commanded the multitude to sit down on the ground.

And he took the seven loaves and the fishes, and gave thanks, and broke them, and gave to his disciples, and the disciples to the multitude. And they all ate and were satisfied, and they picked up what was left over of the broken pieces, seven large baskets full.

✴ BLACK SOCKETED, BLIND ✴

BRIDGES
Psychiatric Wellness Solutions

Journaling Therapy IV: *Tell us about your mother.* (10 Wellness Points™)

Name: <u>Laura Freedman</u>

Most of this is hearsay: she died when I was four. My memories are a tangled net of trash on the shores of consciousness: sea glass, a tennis shoe, an empty bottle, driftwood. After she died, I studied photos, tracing the etiology of her unmaking, so what seems to be a shard of memory may be imaginative gloss caked around a snapshot—maybe I don't remember her at all.

1.

My mother taking a sick chicken to a tree stump, putting it out of its misery with an AXE.

2.

My mother, staring straight at her reflection in the bathroom mirror, washing blood and feathers from her hands.

3.

My mother whirling me around in the yard by my chubby arms while I cackled, until my ankle smacked a tree trunk and I howled.

4.

My mother with a migraine, nailing towels over our windows, screaming at me to shut up as she stuffed rags under the door.

5.

My mother, inhaling chemicals in the toilet bowl, collapsing against the toilet seat, chin bruising blue.

6.

My mother writing me letters from the hospital, letters that grew progressively stranger . . . *Take out my eyes, let me wander black socketed, blind. I will have stones for eyes, stones seal a tomb, and none shall roll it back for what is in there is long dead, and will not, like Lazarus, rise . . .*

7.

My mother coming back from the hospital, passive and dazed.

8.

My mother lying on her back on the sidewalk, glassy-eyed, muttering to herself, while I paced around the lemon tree, doing spells with a stick.

9.

My mother holding my hand at the river as floodwaters receded. My mother stalking shores coated with faded basketballs, pilly tires, battered mesquite branches. My mother poking through tangled stacks of brittle driftwood sticks for bottles sloshing with rotten liquid. My mother lining bottles along the shore. Handing me a rock.

10.

My mother, who made herself a black hole with a piece of frayed rope. My mother, who slipped through the hole and left us circling the void she made.

11.

An eternity on the event horizon, winding after her.

12.

My mother, the bright-plumaged bird who came to my window, who said to me: leave here, before you are destroyed.

✯ THE WORMHOLE ✯

Dear Janice Gibbs,

Here is my submission to *El Giraffe*. "Gruesome Horrors to Whisper in the Dusk" is a series of soul-chilling tales containing beneficial lessons for students such as ourselves. I know that you have high expectations and exacting standards: after all, *El Giraffe* used to be two pages bound with staples, and now that you are Editor-in-Chief, it is fifteen pages bound with string. This year I bet people might start to like it, or even read it, especially if it has tales that glue people to their desks with suspense. Such as the first story in the *Gruesome* series: "The Ghost in the Wall."

A brief summary: a girl named Janice (her having the same name as you is purely of coincidence) moves into a new home with her family. At night, she hears this ghostly scratching in the wall. Her mom says, "It's just a rat honey, and on a totally unrelated note, did you know that the woman who used to live here died of poison oak rash? She scratched herself to death in a tub full of calamine lotion." That night Janice hears the scratching again, and when she wakes up there's a message carved into the wall: I'VE BEEN WATCHING YOU. Janice totally freaks, but her mom just accuses her of writing it herself for the sake of being weird. The next night, the scratching gets louder, and there's this faint smell of calamine lotion. In the morning, Janice summons all her courage and looks at the writing. The message: I'VE BEEN WATCHING YOU . . . I THINK THAT YOU ARE COOL!

MORAL: Sometimes a person you reject as a soul-devouring wraith may just be a potential friend who is watching you and thinking good things about you. Perhaps when this person offers you half of his sandwich when you are the only two people on the bus, you should take it and thank him for his generosity, instead of tossing back your hair and looking out the window.

Anyways, that's the story. I thought you might want a summary before reading the following thirty-page version.

Most Sincerely,
Cody Splunk

Student:

Thank you for your submission to EL GIRAFFE. Unfortunately, it does not meet our editorial needs at this time. We encourage you to keep our magazine in mind in the future, or an even better idea is that you look into a different hobby, such as sports.

Sincerely,
The Editors

Dear Janice Gibbs,

I was so nervous when I found the *El Giraffe* envelope in my locker that I handed it to my best friend, Andy Lopez. He frowned while reading it, then shoved it in the garbage can and said, "That Janice is a bitch." Janice, I want you know that even though Andy Lopez is my best friend, he does not speak for me. I do not think you are a bitch. I just think you have a lot of personality, and that The Sir overreacted to that scissors fight in the bathroom. How were you supposed to know how much that chick's face would bleed? And it's not like you were even dating her boyfriend that long, probably because you realized that he is an asshole and you would be better off with someone who has a more sensitive personality and fewer STDs. The whole situation reminds me of your poem in the last edition of *El Giraffe*, the one called, "Tears of Blood." Some of the lines spoke to me a lot, like: "I had a dream/ and you were there/ you gave me a rose/ I did not care," and, "I plucked one petal from that flower/ You were no longer in my power/ With each petal, a drop of blood/ Added to the swelling flood." I think the flood represents Jesus. Anyways, I know that you have been kicked off the *El Giraffe* staff because of your suspension, but I think this is an injustice because you should still be editor, and I will continue sending my stories to you as a form of protest.

This one is called, "The Yellow Fannypack." It is about a girl who constantly sports a yellow fannypack. Every day her best friend is all: "Why not remove that luminous yellow fannypack?" And she's all: "Sentimental value." Then they grow up and he proposes and they get married. On their wedding night, he's all: "If you love me, you'll finally take off that godforsaken yellow fannypack." "Fine," she says. "If that's what you want." She takes off the fannypack. And HER TORSO FALLS OFF!

In Solidarity,
Cody Splunk

Hi Cody,

Thanks for the note. Not to disillusion you, but I kind of am a bitch. It's nice of you to boycott *El Giraffe* in my honor, but if you ask yourself, "Is it worth it? Will it make a difference?", the answer is probably, "No." So, really. The next time you write a story about a passive-aggressive corpse, send it to them. Not me.

Janice

Dear Janice,

They say that when an editor writes you back a personalized note instead of a photocopied rejection slip, it is a great honor. So, thank you for honoring me. And thanks for encouraging me to keep sending my work to *El Giraffe*. Big news: they are going to publish my story!!! Well, three paragraphs of it. Your replacement, Julie Chang, likes the part which lyrically describes the girl's hair as a river of light through which the boy goes scuba diving.

This triumph is bittersweet. On one hand, I am achieving my dream of publication. But it would mean so much more to me if it was you who had chosen my story. Everyone knows that Julie Chang has low standards, and that she is only on the *El Giraffe* Staff so she can list it on her college applications.

Also, you were only suspended for a week, so I was wondering why you are still not back at school. We miss you!

Your Friend,
Cody

Dear Cody,

It creeps me out that you know where I live, because how else could your letter have gotten into my mailbox? Have you been following me? And have you been wearing a hooded cloak while doing so?

Turns out it wasn't the poor quality of *El Giraffe* submissions that made me throw up every morning, but instead the fact that I am pregnant. Impressive, right? That Danny Ramirez managed to knock up two girls before dropping out to work at the mattress factory? There's even a rumor going around that he got that retarded chick pregnant. She can't really talk though, so they're not sure.

The Holy Mother would disapprove, but I am praying for miscarriage. Do those magic books give you any spells for getting un-impregnated? Do you know about any mushrooms or herbs you can gather? Maybe you can build a time machine. Kidding! I am getting kind of desperate though. I can't go back to school. I feel like I am losing my mind.

Janice

Dear Janice,

I am honored that you would enlist my assistance in resolving your plight. In terms of time-machine building materials, I have a broken radio, three hard drives I salvaged from the dump, unlimited wire, and a power drill. This is unfortunate, because according to science I need a wormhole situated next to a neutron star. Even if I enlisted my brother Greebo's welding skills, we would be out of luck.

Still, I got to thinking. If I could actually make you a time machine, it would be very dangerous. One miscalculation, and you'd get sucked into a black hole. Also, what if you were able to go back in time, say, a year? What would you do? Appear to your past self and say: "Staaaay Awaaaay Frommmm Daaaannnnnyyyyyy"? *Kill* him? And wouldn't you already have a memory of it happening? Anyways, as a matter of chivalry, I would insist on being the one to do the time travelling. But if I appeared to you a year ago and told you not to date Danny, I don't think you would listen. I tried to talk to you all the time last year, and you acted like you didn't hear me. You didn't even notice when I left a box of Girl Scout cookies on your desk on Valentine's Day. You just left them there, and Mrs. Simmons ate them.

In the meantime, I think you should come back to school. I won't tell anyone you're pregnant. And if you're serious about not being pregnant anymore, I can borrow Greebo's car and drive you to Planned Parenthood. It would not be a problem at all.

Your Friend,
Cody

P.S. And I'll keep working on the time machine!

Yo, Cody—

That is really sweet of you to offer to drive me to Planned Parenthood. I would appreciate that.

Does next Friday work for you? You would have to skip school, but I figure you're smart enough to miss one day.

Your Friend,
Janice

Hey Janice—

Friday's totally fine. I have a physics test, but Mrs. Rivas likes me a lot, so I'm sure she'll let me re-take it on Monday.

Wow! I can't believe that in just one week, we have a date! Exciting! I'll keep working on the time machine though, just in case.

:) *Cody*

Cody, you blockhead:

Driving someone to get an abortion is not a DATE.
Alright?

Janice

Dear Janice,

Of course I only meant date as in, like, calendar-appointment. Poor word choice on my part! It's just I have just been so distracted with this time machine business—today I calibrated the radio to intercept a signal from back in time. For 52 seconds, it was working. Then I realized it was just the oldies station.

Aware of appropriate boundaries,
Cody

Hey Dumbfuck—

How retarded do you think I am? Granted, when you showed up at my window at 3:00AM this morning, waving your arms and saying you were my unborn child, time travelling from the year 2026, sent to tell me not to terminate you because you turned out really fun and cool, there was a glint of a moment where I was like, wait! For real? Then I noticed that in an attempt to look futuristic, you had taped tinfoil to your sweatpants. God, Cody. If you don't think I should go through with this, how bout you don't offer to drive me to the clinic. I'll take the fucking bus.

Dear Janice,

Okay, I'm really sorry I attempted to deceive you. It's just I told my older sister I needed Greebo's car so I could offer you taxi service on Friday, and she said that she got rid of a baby her Sophomore year. That was when she got really depressed and grew her hair down over her face and dropped out to work at the chicken shack. I didn't want that to happen to you.
I'll still drive you if you want.

Sorry,
Cody

Dear Janice,

I understand why you didn't reply to my last letter. Still, it's good to see you back in school. Also, the gossip on the yearbook staff is that after a brief power struggle, you regained your rightful standing as Editor-in-Chief of *El Giraffe*. I was so glad to hear that. I saw you laughing at lunchtime, sitting at the back table with your friends. I guess you went ahead and took care of your problem. I'm glad to see you're not all depressed. You are a good person. I want you to be happy.

Your friend,
Cody

Dear Janice,

Okay, I get the picture. You didn't have to give me back all my letters. They were yours to keep.

I don't know why I'm even
sending this,
Cody

Dear Janice,

It was really unnecessary to have The Sir sit me down for a conversation about stalking. In fact, it was mean. You know, he was going to write me a scholarship recommendation letter for college. What's he going to say now? "Cody is a kind person and very bright in science, math, and writing, but like everyone he has his flaws, such as being a stalker?"

My last letter EVER!
Cody

Dear *El Giraffe* editors,

This is an anonymous submission, entitled, "The Wormhole."

Signed,
Anonymous

The Wormhole

Once upon a time there was a boy who loved a girl who did not love him back. The boy did his best to woo her, with words and chivalrous deeds. In these attempts he was overzealous—he alienated the girl entirely, and she refused to look upon his face.

The boy wanted a do-over, so he got a job as the night janitor at NASA. He studied the stars, mapping the sky, searching for black holes and neutron stars. After years of calculation, he re-programmed NASA's most promising spaceship, and shot himself towards the black hole at the center of our galaxy. A wormhole spat him out, and his spaceship splashed into the ocean. After floating in an escape pod for several days, he was hauled aboard a freighter ship. "What year is it?" he demanded. "2072," a tattooed sailor said.

It was the same year he'd left. *I may as well jump back into the ocean*, he thought. What the old man didn't realize was that his calculations were mistaken. Instead of sending him back in time, the wormhole sent him to a parallel universe. As fate would have it, this was the universe in which the girl loved him back.

When the ship got to shore, the old man realized he was not, in fact, in his own world. So he tracked down his parallel universe self. His doppelganger was sitting on a porch swing in Montana, holding hands with the girl, who had been his wife for fifty years. They were drinking lemonade and watching their grandchildren play in the yard. The old man stood in the cornfields, absorbing the family happiness of his twin.

He considered murdering his doppelganger and slipping into his place. He could play tiddlywinks with his grandchildren; sleep each night next to the woman he loved. It would be easy. He'd dig a deep hole. Bonk his second self on the head with a shovel. Steal his clothes. Push the body into the pit, shovel dirt on his face.

No, the old man thought. He turned, and wandered out toward the open road. *It is enough to know that among the infinity of universes, one contained for me a chance at love.*

✯ THE HOLY INNOCENT ✯

There is something silent and filled with sunlight about this bathroom, maybe because you are alone in it, and you can breathe. Creamy white paint has been smeared along the sides of the window and over the metal crank that opens it. You twirl the crank open and look out at the decaying stucco houses and the empty fields beyond.

There are bits of glue stuck to your fingers, from making construction paper bookmarks with spaz-brains from H wing. You look down at the glue on your skin and remember youth group, when you used to smear glue on your hands and let it dry, then peel it off in flakes.

In the church basement, you used to make these tattoos on yourself. You tipped backwards in your chair on the thick pea-green carpet, writing on your wrist while Sister Gloria sketched non-violent communication spheres on the chalkboard. The first time you smoked with Danny, he licked his thumb, and rubbed it on your wrist.

"You don't have paper, there, or what?"

You shook your head, watching mallards stick their beaks down in the muck for weeds and worms.

Stupid Danny. He worked at the discount mattress factory. His boss wouldn't let him rip off mattress-tags in the warehouse, so he cut the tags off of everything else: your sweater, your book bag, your underwear.

You unbutton your jeans and sit down on the cool porcelain, looking at your tattered, scribbled-on high tops. They are the shoes you were wearing when you found out about the baby, from a test kit you bought on the way home from school. A baby in your belly, you'd thought, looking at the tab coming up blue for positive. An uninvited guest, unfurling in your stomach like a weed, a vine, a tree.

"I did not invite you to grow here," you'd said to it, tracing your finger across your belly. "I did not invite you in."

You took the baby to see all of the things in your life you wanted to show it: through the lining of your belly. You walked with the baby through the rutted, unplanted fields, you showed the baby: these are clods of dirt that grow in the sun, these are the white worms that squeeze their way up from the earth. These are the grasses by the creek. You showed your baby the secret places that only you know.

Your baby. You showed it your world and then you said: Out with you. Enough. You are out of here, you nosy little thing, I did not invite you here, get out—you fungus, you infection. I am giving you nothing, you said—touching your belly—you little mist of yeast, you rabbit, you grub, curled up with a big head like a walnut. And the baby went. You starved the little fucker out.

When you stopped eating, things slowed down. You slowed down too. You sat at your desk and you sat up as straight as you could. You sat up as tall as you could. You were waving back and forth. You drifted away on a plank and nobody knew this, which was fine, because it was your secret. It was for you to know and for no other person to know. You had a pain in your gut when it started, the baby coming out. Sharp pain like the first time you got your period, and you tried not to crumple over. You raised your hand to get out of the classroom, to go and sit in the cool bathroom stall and let it out. But when you stood up, you fainted. Then they gathered around you, and you peered up at them, like trees in the sun.

You pull up your pants and button them and bust open the bathroom door. Gazing down the empty blue-carpeted hallways, you decide to go and check on Helen, in the B wing. You need to kill an hour before you go home to your aunt's house, where you've lived since your Dad got transferred to Kentucky. Your dad worked as a mechanic on the line at the Smucker's plant, and he used to bring home little packets of grape and strawberry jam, the kind you get with your breakfast at Denny's when you order toast. Now your dad mails you shoebox packages with actual jars of jam wrapped in Styrofoam peanuts, on Christmas and your birthday. When you were twelve, you used to eat jam with spoons for breakfast and tuck lumps of it in your sandwiches at lunch. Now you hate jam. You hate its slimy sweetness; you hate how it has no flavor or bite. You'd rather have dry naked bread, hard-crusted, chalky-making to your mouth. The sweetness of your own spit is better than your father's stupid jam. You don't tell your Dad this, of course, you don't tell Dad anything. Really, you never did. He was always preoccupied, silent, nothing you said ever seemed to really go into his head.

Helen's room is at the end of the "B" wing. Her nephew pays extra for her to have a single, plus pockets of special attention time from the aides. Helen weighs three hundred and seventy-two pounds, and she cannot move by herself, except for her left arm.

You knock before entering her room. It is dark and silent. A breeze flaps at the curtains, and they rustle against the sill.

"Helen?" you whisper. She is sitting in her Lay-Z-Boy with eyes half-closed, throat gurgling, and you can't tell if she's sleeping or awake.

Her eyes flap open. "Janice," she croaks hoarsely. "I need . . . to pee."

Your timing, as always, is dead-center wrong. You wheel over the automatic lift machine and hook her hulking body into it, press the button to lift her up and set her on her plastic wheelchair toilet.

Man, you think to yourself, as you step outside her room, giving her a sliver of privacy. You lean against the wall with your arms folded, already hearing the tinkling and plopping. You look down at your shoes.

Really—it was better for your baby not to be born, then, with the kind of life it would have had. You could not hide a baby where you hid the other things, in the toe of your sneaker, in a box on the top shelf of your closet. No.

Your baby can come back to your womb another time, its soul can come back later, when you are older. When you have left this town, when you have left this state, when you have a shady tomato garden and chimes on your porch. You will be one of those older pregnant women with fine muscles and sun-browned skin. Your baby will grow inside you again, bright and strong, and it will come out kicking, so glad you made it wait.

But maybe it doesn't work like that, with souls and all. Maybe your baby just went to limbo, and is stuck there forever.

"Janice," Helen croaks from inside her room. You hoist her back up from the toilet with the machine. It's strange to lift a person up like that, to lift a dead weight of a person with a machine. You wipe her soft hanging ass and replace her diaper with a new one, sticking on the plastic tabs. Then you pull her black stretch sweat pants up and set her back down in her chair. You rinse out the removable bucket from her wheelchair toilet, running water over it in her tiny bathroom, looking at the glass bottle of sand from Florida perched on the windowsill.

You think of when Sister Gloria brought your youth group to the beach. It was the day after you took the pregnancy test, and you hadn't eaten anything for dinner the night before, or lunch that day. The sky was shining pink against the water, eddies of foam were rushing and crashing beneath the wind. There had been a storm, and the dunes were peeled bare by sweeping storm waves.

The other kids were running around in the uprushing froth of waves, rolling up the legs of their pants, throwing sandballs. Sister Gloria stood next to you on the sand, taking off her high-waisted jeans. Underneath, she wore a pilly black bathing suit. In that bathing suit, she seemed more naked than anyone you had ever seen. She walked into the water, straight on, up to her waist. Then she just stood there, letting the waves hit her, staring at the trail of light on the water leading out to the sky.

You sat on the sand, tracing a circle around yourself with a piece of drift-wood. You were still deciding what to do. When Sister Gloria turned and came back in from the water, she wrapped herself in a brown towel and sat next to you. The other kids in the youth group were whipping each other with strips of seaweed. There was a dead seal on the beach next to where they were playing, and when they got too close to it, sand flies jumped from its decaying skin.

"Sister Gloria," you said, the wind paring your voice down to softness, "Where does a baby go? When it doesn't get born, I mean."

"Where do you think it might go?"

"Heaven. Right? Like God's sending a baby to hell."

"We can never overestimate God's mercy."

"But the real rules? Like, with the Pope and stuff?"

"Some theologians say that the unborn dead become companion martyrs to the Holy Innocent."

"The Holy Innocent?"

She popped a seaweed pod with her thumb and forefinger. "Are you pregnant, Janice?"

"Sister Gloria! You know I'm not stupid like that."

"Just meditating upon mortality?"

"Yeah. That seal over there is my inspiration."

Companion Martyrs to the Holy Innocent—not such an awful job. And it seemed like with being a nun and all, Sister Gloria would be right.

But Sister Gloria was wrong about a lot of things. You, for instance. She thought that she'd get you out of your mess of a family with beatitudes and liturgical dance, but instead you brought the mess with you. You pierced your belly button with a safety pin in the girl's bathroom, rolled a joint with a page from Deuteronomy, and drank sacramental wine until you threw up in the community garden. You dumped dish soap in the courtyard fountain of the Virgin Mary, and on Halloween you put fake blood running down in tears from her cheeks, so that for two days everyone thought there was a miracle.

"Janice," Helen croaks to you from your chair. You've been spacing out again.

You finish rinsing out the removable toilet-wheelchair bucket, then sit back down on her bed, hands wet.

"So," you say to Helen. "What's up with you?"

Helen sits up slightly in her recliner, her sleep-crusted eyes half-drooping, her mouth open, her wrinkled forearms spotted like toads. Hoarsely, she confides that she finds the weather humid, the Mexican cook erratic with spices, her children neglectful, the staff abusive.

"Hmmm," you say. "That sucks."

While Helen speaks to you about her actress-niece's wedding (held in a theater), you flap through her photo book from her years in a retirement community in Florida. Pretty tame, all of it. Lots of pictures of social hours—tables of brownies, old ladies in dresses, poorly composed shots of condominiums and misty pink sunsets.

You snap the photo book closed and look at the pictures hanging on Helen's wall. One of them is a black-and-white photograph of her youngest daughter. Helen's told you before—she died in a car accident.

"Helen," you say. "What do you think happens to us when we die?"

"The bugs eat us," she croaks.

"You don't believe in heaven and hell?"

"The bugs . . . have to eat something . . . so they . . . eat us." She gestures slightly with the arm she can move, straining.

"Even kids? The bugs get them, too?"

"Everyone," Helen says, her eyes running with intensity.

"But you believe in *souls*. We all have souls."

"No," says Helen, her voice ragged. "When you die . . . you die."

You watch Helen's fish eyes, opened wide, watering in nests of wrinkled skin. "Are you *afraid* of death?" you finally ask.

"No," says Helen. "I wish for it . . . every night." Rivulets of water well from her eyes, and her mouth is gaping open. You don't know what to do.

"Tell me about your daughter," you finally say. You nod at the wall. "The one in that picture on the beach. What was she like?"

"Like you," Helen says.

You look at the picture of the girl. She is standing in a swimsuit at the beach, arms folded, hair wisping out of a bathing cap.

"She had dimples," Helen croaks. "Like you."

You make a corner of your mouth smile, press your hand into your cheek, feel the indentation.

"She was a pistol," Helen says.

"A pistol?"

"You're too good for this place," Helen croaks. "You belong in school."

After clocking out, you walk home—past the bakery that sells *quinceañera* cakes, the discount video palace, the wedding supply store displaying grey-skinned mannequins swathed in gauze. You pass the elementary school where your aunt works. She is home making dinner right now, you know, boiling a pot of chicken. You know that soon you will be sitting on the couch with her, chewing on chicken bones, watching television. You pass the gas station where you stopped this morning and drank three cups of coffee from a paper cup, drank until you could not keep your hand from shaking, until coffee sloshed over the top of your cup onto your fingers.

You cut through the Portuguese cemetery, dragging your feet through gravel, reading names carved in cement. Some barred, raised tombs with diamond-shaped stained glass windows line the part of the cemetery closest to the road. At the far end is a new cement mausoleum. You walk over to inspect it. It is like the cubbies you had in grade school, six coffin-spaces high and wide, waiting for the new dead.

You touch the bottom coffin-slot with your scribbled-on toe. You squat down and lean in. There's a couple of dried oak leaves that have blown inside, and it's kind of damp in the back.

You stick your head further in, stretch your arms out, and wiggle yourself inside. You roll over on your back. You can hardly hear the cars as they rush down the road. The ceiling is a chalky white. It's not so terrible in the tomb, kind of calm and quiet.

The cement is making your shoulder blades cold. It could make all of you cold. If you lay here long enough, you would be paralyzed, nothing in you would move. Then, the worms would come. They would say: we've already met your baby, Janice. And now we are meeting you.

God you say. God. I have something to say to you. Can I have this baby back? Can I have its little soul? God. Please.

You listen.

Nada.

You close your eyes. You set your cold hands under your shirt, shocking the warm skin of your stomach. Through your palms, you can feel your blood moving, your heart beating. Your body: alive.

Your baby will find you. Your baby will find its way back home. You will say: I have made a place for you here. Climb in, my love. Now you will be safe. All is well here, my love, my darling. My darling, my own.

✯ FIRST THE SEA ✯ GAVE UP HER DEAD

BRIDGES

Psychiatric Wellness Solutions

Journaling Therapy V: *While Bridges subscribes to a post-Freudian therapy model, we believe that dream analysis may enable repressed emotions to emerge. Please describe the last dream you can remember.* (10 Wellness Points™)

Name: Laura Freedman

First the sea gave up her dead. They floated upwards in their olden clothes, clammy, the color of clay. We hauled them upwards with nets and laid them on the coral shore. We waited for them to wake up. Rumors of war came from the East. A terrible thing in the water. Nobody wanted to watch as the skin of the earth swelled up like a blister and let what was in there out.

Bones it was. Mostly. We couldn't see them moving, but each day they drew themselves closer to whole creatures, joints meeting and knowing one another as kin. The priest said the earth was tired of people. It was spitting them out like bad fish. Expelling the poison of men.

When our hair grew faster, we knew time was speeding up. The film reel cranked faster to end this ugly picture. A woman gave birth in a cave in the mountains. She was out hunting truffles. She had been only three weeks with child.

I grew breasts and began to bleed. They dressed me in white and tied a list of their sins to my back. They sent me to speak to God. God, who is invisible, prefers no place to another, but is equally distributed within each grain and drop. I sat on the beach and picked a green leaf from a green plant. I spoke to God in the leaf. "You who can do all things," I said. "We would like more time." The leaf said nothing. Or maybe it said everything, which, as all colors make white, sounds like nothing. On the beach, the dead were moaning. I watched them rise. The trees pulled themselves from the ground and walked hand in hand with the dead. There was nothing to do but follow.

I held the leaf in my pocket. When we reached the center of everything, the dead called out to God. I raised up my hand. The leaf was dry and gray. "Sheep and Goats," I said. "Separate." The trees knew they were good. The people were more shy. "How do we know?" they asked.

"Everyone is welcome," I said. "And there will be no more time."

✮ MEXICO FOXTROT RIDES AGAIN ✮

FROM: splunkmiester@yahoo.com
TO: janthepiratespy@hotmail.com
SUBJECT: EMERGENCY!!! ALERT!!!!

Dear Janice,

Terrible news: Ms. Freedman is being held against her will in an INSANE ASYLUM!
We must rescue her before she is lobotomized! I have the keys to Greebo's car, a
map of Austin, and a crowbar. I need an accomplice on this journey, and as Andy
Lopez is at tuba camp, YOU ARE MY ONLY HOPE.

> Urgently,
> Cody

P.S. How are you doing? What is new with you? I am starting at Texas Tech in the
fall! I am super excited!

FROM: janthepiratespy@hotmail.com
TO: splunkmiester@yahoo.com
SUBJECT: RE: EMERGENCY!!! ALERT!!!

Hey Cody,

Just so you know, your e-mail made you sound a little crazy. Life tip: avoid writing
in all caps. It puts people off.

While I'm aware that Ms. Freedman is in a nut ward, I'm skeptical about the lobotomy. And what makes you think she's being held against her will? I admit that from the website, the place seems new age and creepy. I do kind of wonder why she hasn't written back to my emails for like a year. I'm pretty sure they're giving her electro-shocks . . .

God, maybe you're right. Not about the lobotomy, but about her being kind of trapped there. Maybe we do need to go rescue her. I mean, not really rescue her. But just check in?

~Janice

Jailbreak!
A True History by Cody Splunk

The day dawned coarse and muggy, red sun on the rise. Red sun means bloodshed, my father always said. I took a final drag on my fizzy caffeine pick-me-up. Swearing an oath that the blood would be that of our enemies, I crumpled the can in my fist.

With a sudden, jarring, door slam, my partner in crime emerged from her abode, almond eyes flashing, black hair twisting in the breeze. Janice was a full plate of spaghetti—personality for five packed into one supple frame. And yet: her Yeti jeans had loosened since I'd seen her last. She was all angles. I added a secondary mission to the quest-o-meter: fatten Janice up. Fifteen minutes into our drive, I swerved into a Dr. Butterbeans.

"Just coffee," Janice said, lighting a cigarette.

I ordered two extra-large breakfast specials.

"Sure that's healthy, Splunk?"

Driving with one hand, I tossed breakfast in her lap. "Something to soak up the coffee."

Janice stared at the bacon cool ranch burrito, then flung it out the window. "I have a problem," she said, as it splattered against a fire hydrant.

"Apparently."

She took a yellow notebook from her bag. *Laura's Journal of Mystery and Wonder*, the cover read.

"*You* stole it?"

An open case, closed—with my partner in crime the culprit.

"It was Danny."

"Of course." Danny, the perpetual villain, always managed to slip through the fingers of the law. "When?"

"That day Gasher got his hand stuck in the computer screen."

Chaos—a perfect cover for crime.

"How'd you get it from Danny?"

"It was under his mattress."

"You're still seeing him?"

"What's it to you?"

"He treated you like shit, madam."

"I treated you like shit, sir."

"You were going through a hard time."

"That's no excuse." Janice extinguished her cigarette on her shoe. We passed a billboard that read: HELL IS REAL.

"So how's the rest home?"

"I wouldn't put my hamster there."

"You have a hamster?"

"They fired me. For smoking patients' cigarettes."

"Harsh."

"Well, I also ate one lady's diazepam."

"That's like a German sweetbread?"

"It's more like valium."

"So does Freedman know you have her journal?"

"Dude, I got it yesterday."

I swerved, almost veering into a ditch. "You were with Danny *last night*?"

"Cody! You are not my boyfriend!"

"Is Danny?"

"None of your business.

"You're throwing your life away like a rancid pot of stew!"

"And you, my friend, are a terrible driver."

I steadied the vehicle. We passed a porno store. Lurid posters obscured the windows. 24-Hour DVD! TRUCKERS WELCOME!!!

"Anyway," Janice said. "Fill me in on the genius rescue plan."

"Behind you."

Janice turned around in her seat, inspecting my array of supplies. "You recently join the circus?"

"Those are our disguises. You're going to wear the wig, sunglasses, and raincoat."

"Is the plan that I expose myself on a playground?"

"When they bring Ms. Freedman out to see us, we communicate our plan through morse code blinking."

"Ms. Freedman knows morse code?"

"She's been to college."

"Where she studied *literature*."

"You and Ms. Freedman trade outfits in the bathroom. You remain hidden in the stall. Wearing your clothes, Ms. Freedman accompanies me from the building."

"How long do I have to stay in the insane asylum toilet stall?"

"That's where the rope ladder comes in. Once we clear the premises, the security system should be disabled by the super-virus I loaded onto the mainframe."

"This is crazy."

"Yes," I said. "Crazy enough to work."

A wooden sign shaped like the golden gate bridge announced our destination. "*Bridges*," it read. "*Psychiatric Wellness Solutions*." The blacktop road ended in a baking-hot parking lot. Janice jumped out of the car and stretched, riding-up tee shirt revealing starving-horse ribs. I donned a fedora, and tossed her the raincoat. "Showtime, sister."

We followed a red brick walk past low-slung stucco buildings and a tennis court with faded lines. In a fenced-in swim area, a maintenance man fished a dead mouse from the hot tub.

"Remind me to skip the jacuzzi," Janice muttered.

Inside, the air conditioning made a white-noise roar. At the nurse's station, a man typed intently. We studied the glossy printout tacked to the bulletin board above his head.

WEEKLY WELLNESS POINTS™ MEMO

Due to recent events, WELLNESS POINTS™ penalties have been expanded. Time to TAKE RESPONSIBLILTY™, folks. You have no one to blame but yourselves.

Poking an orderly in the belly and
shouting, "You are plump and good for
Eating!"   -10 Wellness Points™

Pretending to be deaf, and, when docked
Wellness Points™, filing a complaint under
the "Americans with Disabilities Act."   -25 Wellness Points™

Attempting to wager Sexual Favors
On Casino Night   -35 Wellness Points™

Starting "cells" of a "Communist Party" to overthrow
the capitalist system of cognitive-behavioral therapy.   -50 Wellness Points™

Nailing Dr. Sherman Weir in the eye
with a paper airplane, that, when
unfolded, says "FUCK YOU, Dr. Bin Ladin."   -75 Wellness Points™

"Villagers are restless." Janice pushed her sunglasses up on her nose and
tapped the bell.

The bearded orderly stood, frizzy hair on end. "How may I help you?"

We're here to visit Laura Freedman," Janice said.

"I guess you should sign in the 'ol binder. Would you like a complimentary
Bridges: Psychiatric Wellness Solutions golf pencil?"

"Absolutely," Janice said.

We signed in.

The orderly glanced at the binder and raised his eyebrows. "I'll let Laura
know that Kristi Colimote and *Mexico Foxtrot* are here to see her," he said,
disappearing into the back room.

Janice kicked me. "Nice code name. Subtle."

"Okay." Beardo called back to us. "Visitor's area down the hall and to the
right."

The visiting room smelled like antiseptic solution. Ms. Freedman was
escorted in by an orderly in a fauxhawk. Her hair was in a weird wadded up
bun on her head, and her tee shirt was emblazoned with paw prints and red
letters that read: MY CAT WALKS ALL OVER ME. "Janice? Cody?" She
sank into a folding chair and pinched my arm. "Is this really happening?"

"We thought you were lobotomized," Janice said.

"Not yet." She gave a brittle laugh. "Ever since the Fudgesicle incident,
though, they stopped giving me your letters."

"I'm starting at Texas Tech in the fall," I said.

"Congratulations."

"I can make four types of breakfast burritos," Janice said.

"Oh?"

"I work at Circle K." Janice said. "I didn't really graduate. I never got my PE credits."

Ms. Freedman suddenly looked like herself again: sober. Exhausted. "Janice." She put her head in her hands. "I blame myself."

"That's funny," Janice said, "Because I blame Cody."

"I blame Society," I said.

"I blame God," Janice said. "Who made the world, anyway?"

"The big bang," I said.

"Yet you believe in dragons," Janice said.

We sat there for a moment.

"Where are my manners!" Ms. Freedman suddenly exclaimed. "May I offer you a snack?" She removed a napkin wrapped packet from her pocket, peeled back a rubber band, and proffered a smashed cookie.

"Thanks," Janice said, taking a piece. She chewed. "Oh my God." She spat into her hand. "That's so incredibly stale."

Ms. Freedman's pale fingers tightened around the napkin.

"Ms. Freedman," Janice said. "We're here to spring you."

"I don't know about that, Wellness Points™ wise," Ms. Freedman said. "Bad debt, you know. Credit score."

"Ms. Freedman, use your critical thinking skills." Janice said.

"Like we practiced with the toothpaste ads," I said.

Ms. Freedman's eyes welled with tears.

I glanced at the fauxhawked orderly, who was dozing in his chair. "Smoke bombs at the ready," I said.

Janice took Ms. Freedman's hand, yanked slightly. Ms. Freedman stood. Haltingly, she followed Janice into the bathroom. I scouted the premises, fingering my nunchucks. Then I pressed my ear to the bathroom door. Ms. Freedman and Janice were speaking earnestly.

"I starved it out," Janice was saying. "I killed it."

"Janice. It is not medically possible to starve a baby out."

"It worked, though."

"Spontaneous miscarriage is extremely common in the first trimester. Especially with a first pregnancy."

"It would be one month old."

There was a pause.

"I'm so sorry, Janice."

"Hey. Don't start crying on me, Miss."

"Emotional lability. Minus 10 Wellness Points™."

"Anyway, your make-up's done. You look kind of good with that wig on."

"This is crazy."

"Yes." Janice swung the bathroom door open. "Crazy enough to work."

In the raincoat, sunglasses and wig, Ms. Freedman looked like a sad clown. She rubbed her eyes, smudging eyeliner. "How's Janice escaping?" she whispered.

"I've got pepper spray and a rope ladder."

"Janice." Ms. Freedman set her hands on Janice's shoulders. "I need you to promise you won't assault anyone. Aggressive Aggression is minus 100 Wellness Points™."

"Scout's honor."

"Janice will run down the highway to the gas station," I said. "Once she's there, she'll radio in. We'll swing back and pick her up."

"And get Slurpees," Janice added.

"I haven't had a Slurpee in *years*," Ms. Freedman said.

"Alright, Ms. Freedman." I took her hand. "Here goes nothing."

Schizophrenics shuffled past, minds wrapped in terrible cocoons. Ms. Freedman didn't seem to know what to do with her hands. "Do you have a cell phone?" she whispered.

I handed her my phone. Ms. Freedman held it to hear ear. "No, Gretchen," she said, animated. "I can't give you a better offer on the house." Walking aggressively, she made a beeline for the door.

I moseyed up to Beardo at the front desk. "Can I sign us both out?" I asked. I nodded to Ms. Freedman, who had her back to us. "My girlfriend's on an important phone call."

Beardo gazed out the window at Ms. Freedman's back. "You know," he said. "Your girlfriend's ankles remind me of Laura's ankles. Such slender, delicate, ankles."

"Your commentary seems inappropriate."

"Is it alright if I step outside and say goodbye to—what was her name—

Kristi Colimote? Beardo tucked the binder under his arm. "She really should sign the binder."

"Sir," I said, blocking his way. "It's a very important phone call."

Beardo stared me down. "Is it, *Mexico Foxtrot*?"

I blinked.

"Emilia," Beardo called into the back room. "Situation 2."

A rotund woman in pink scrubs emerged from the back room. "Situation 2," she barked into the intercom. Classical music started up on the PA system.

I glanced behind me. Ms. Freedman was nowhere to be seen. I made a break for the front door. As I pushed it open, I shouted, "Run for it, Ms. F!"

"I'm going after him," Beardo screamed, flinging himself at the door.

I sprinted down the red brick path, then veered left, into a courtyard filled with tiny fountains. I tore around a shed, Beardo's footsteps pounding gravel behind me. I faked a right, then sprinted across a sand garden to the parking lot, jabbing my hand into my pocket for the keys. Beardo made a dive for my feet, pulled my ankles out from under me. "Where is she, you bastard?" he shouted, sitting on my back, wrenching my arm. "Where is she?" I raised my bleeding face and scanned the parking lot. Greebo's car was gone.

Janice and I sat in dark leather chairs of Dr. Sherman Weir's office, hands tied behind our backs.

Dr. Weir wore a red bow tie and sported a luxuriant mustache. He paced the room, piercing us with a steely gaze.

"Let me guess," Janice said. "You have ways of making us talk."

Dr. Weir opened a desk drawer, removed an inkblot flash card. "Tell me," he said. "What do you see?"

"Your mom's honeypot," Janice said.

Dr. Weir flicked the flashcard like a throwing star. It stuck up out of the carpet. "Where's Laura?" he demanded. "Where is she?"

"I have literally no clue, sir. She actually stole my car."

"We were just visiting, sir. You have no right to detain us."

Dr. Weir sat on the edge of his desk, arms crossed. "According to one Max Gusterson, Laura Freedman was wearing the clothing you came in with." He poked Janice lightly on the forehead.

"Get your hands off her!" I cried.

"Listen," Janice said. "We want lawyers."

Dr. Weir laughed maniacally. "This isn't a police station. You have no rights. I've checked you in as patients."

"Patients have rights," Janice said. "In the nursing home, there was an eldercare ombudsman."

"We demand to speak to your ombudsman," I roared.

"There is no ombudsman." Dr. Weir laughed. "The complaint line goes directly to me. And complaints have a way of . . . disappearing."

Janice raised her eyebrows. "Minus a million Wellness Points for being batshit crazy."

Dr. Weir looked stricken.

"You have so many bats in your belfry they violated the building code!" I said, snapping my neck aggressively.

Janice glanced at me, confused.

"From overcrowding. Because there were so many bats!"

Dr. Weir cleared his throat. "You should know, munchkins, that you have deprived us of a very lucrative patient. Ms. Freedman was participating in an important medical trial. The pharmaceutical company will be quite disappointed." He shook his head. "If only we had a replacement." He set his hands on Janice's shoulders. "You wanted to be Laura Freedman? Congratulations. You *are* Laura Freedman."

"Oh yeah?" Janice said. "I don't even have insurance."

I struggled to free my wrists. "Our parents will come looking for us! We'll expose your conspiracy!"

Dr. Weir flipped through papers on a clipboard. "Let's see." He nodded at Janice. "Oppositional-defiant disorder, *anorexia nervosa*." He pointed at me. "Mania. Delusions of grandeur." He set the clipboard on the table. "Oh, nurse," he called musically. "Will you ready the Thorazine?"

Beardo stepped in with a tray full of needles, grinning.

"Now are you sure you don't want to tell me where our patient is?" Dr. Weir demanded.

Beardo readied the needle at my shoulder.

"Never," I spat.

The door flew open, kicked in by a canvas high top. Ms. Freedman stood in the doorway, wielding an X-ACTO knife.

Dr. Weir's mouth fell open.

Moving like lightning, Ms. Freedman jabbed the Thorazine into Beardo's thigh. He crumpled to the ground. She wrestled Dr. Weir into a headlock and held the needle to his throat. "Time for a taste of your own medicine," she whispered, and drove the needle home. He sank to the plush red carpet. "Sleeping on the job," she muttered. "Minus 50 Wellness Points™."

She slashed the X-ACTO knife across our bonds, then looped the rope ladder around a desk leg. "What do you think, kids?" Her eyes were wild; her makeup smeared like war paint. "Time to check out?"

We scrambled down a brambly hillside, where Greebo's car sat waiting in the Circle K parking lot. We bought three extra-large Slurpees, filled the tank with gas, and floored it into Austin.

Ms. Freedman's brother lived in a high-rise apartment. We paused before it, engine running.

"Well," she said, looking small and tired in the back seat. "I'm going to have a lot of questions to answer. I think I'd better go in alone."

We nodded.

"Thanks for rescuing me," she said. "I don't know how I can thank you." Tears ran down her cheeks. "I wasn't even a very good teacher."

"Yes you were," Janice said.

"You were just different," I said.

Ms. Freedman smiled sadly.

"Good luck, Ms. Freedman," Janice said.

Ms. Freedman turned, walked up the path, and pressed the buzzer. As the front door opened, it bathed her in a frame of light.

Back on the highway, it was a long time before we talked. "You didn't give the journal back," I finally said.

"No shit."

"You chicken out?"

Janice unrolled the window, letting cool air rush in. She pulled the journal out of her bag, pressed on the overhead light.

"Janice Gibbs: a feral child with excessive eye shadow and stringy black hair that obscures her face. I feel a daily urge to take scissors to it. She has an anti-authoritarian complex that would be interesting were it not so ill informed."

"Ouch."

"Yeah. But, obviously that's not how she always felt. Otherwise she wouldn't have even kept in touch, you know?"

"I guess."

"I think it's better if she doesn't know that I know she thought I was a little shit. I mean, before she knew me."

"Good call."

Janice switched on the radio, and we sang along really loud with the windows open.

It was pretty much the best night of my life.

THE END

FROM: janthepiratespy@hotmail.com
TO: splunkmeister@yahoo.com
SUBJECT: collective memory

Hey there Cody,

I read your account of our adventure with much interest. However, I remember a few things a bit differently. For instance, if memory serves me correctly, after we went up to Ms. Freedman's room, she shared that she was going to be released in two weeks. She checked out on a day pass, and we ate lunch at Burger King. Then we dropped her off at her brother's house.

I'm doing night shifts at the Circle K on North 23rd street. Stop by sometime for Funyuns. We'll catch up.

Your pal,

Janice

✳ THEIR TRUNKS ✳ WERE THEIR HANDLES

Sitting on the cold cement, Janice felt foreign to herself. A thousand years away from any city she had known. Maybe by city she meant her childhood. She could say, "We had these plastic elephant cups, one blue, one pink, their trunks were their handles." She could say that to Juan, and he would look at her, waiting for the rest of the story. Juan didn't understand. The elephant cups were a story in themselves.

Juan had the shift before her, and she would burble up with stories to make him stay longer, grabbing at thoughts like fish in a stream, blurting them out in fluorescent light. She didn't like to be in there alone in her green vest, passing cigarettes over the ad-emblazoned counter to skinny users who radiated sharp sparks of need.

She had not been a user herself, not really, not until a junkie threw a cup of boiling coffee at her face just as she was ringing up his purchase. Reeling from forming blisters, she had tripped on a box of pineapple rings, jerked something in her back. The junkie peeled all the green from the register, was out before she called 911. When the doctor stopped refilling her Percoset, she got it from a neighbor with a plastic hip. Her aunt thought she slept with the dude to get the pills, but Jesus. She had standards. Leaning on a metal bat, her aunt rang the dude's doorbell and said: keep it up and you'll have plastic elbows. In the doorway, Janice sank to the tile in laughter. *Plastic elbows.*

Her aunt stood over her, bat raised.

Go ahead, Janice said. I dare you.

Her aunt dropped the bat, sat on the couch, turned on the television. Janice got up and made instant mashed potatoes. In the glare of the flashing screen, they spooned hot, milky, ketchup-slathered bites to their mouths.

At work that night, she slipped a fifty up her sleeve.

Stupid.

Stupid.

Stupid.

The holding pen was the size of a cramped kitchenette. There was a drinking fountain with a clogged drain spilling water on cement, a metal toilet bolted to a back wall. Janice shifted her weight from foot to foot.

"Knew I'd end up here," muttered a heavy woman with a straw-colored braid. She wore a shirt that read: EVIL KEEPS ME YOUNG.

"I have that shirt," Janice said.

"I didn't realize it came in 'Elvin.'"

"I didn't realize it came in 'Elephant.'"

"You're sweating. You should take off your jacket."

"You should take off your face." A sharp pain tore through Janice's lower intestine. She bit her lip until it bled.

The large woman lowered her voice. "Are you a vampire?"

"What gave me away?"

"Bloody teeth. I'm Gwen, by the way."

"Zelda of the Night."

"Want to know what I'm in for?"

"Desperately."

"I took my daughter to McDonalds."

"Didn't realize that was illegal in Texas."

"Apparently it's kidnapping."

"Yikes."

"Yeah, well, when your baby gets ripped out of your arms and adopted by a rich bitch who sends you pictures every year, then calls and says your nine-year-old daughter wants to meet you, and you drive three hours every month to eat a Happy Meal with her, that does NOT give you the right to pick her up from school and take her to McDonalds yourself. Apparently that's kidnapping." She slammed her head against the wall. Hard.

"Jesus."

Gwen leveled her face at Janice. "I have multiple chemical imbalances."

"Go figure."

"All my hair fell out when I was four. From stress. My mom's boyfriend would chase me around the house pretending to be a gremlin."

"Sounds stressful."

"The doctors were really surprised when it grew back."

"Move it, *Mija*." An emaciated woman in heavy makeup slapped Gwen's shoulder. "I have bad knees," she explained, sinking down and sighing.

"What are you in for?" Gwen asked.

"I ran over my husband."

In the corner, a toothless woman gave a sharp staccato laugh.

"He deserved it."

"Obviously," Gwen said.

"After twenty years of marriage. I should have known from the start. I hated my wedding."

"How come?" Gwen asked.

"It was a terrible day. Before, I didn't get my period for three months."

"You were pregnant?" Janice asked.

"I was a virgin."

"Hey, I know all about pregnant virgins," Gwen said.

"I was an Ivory girl. Twenty-two years old. 98% pure."

"Keep your feet in a bucket and a penny between your knees!" the toothless woman screamed.

"And then, I got it the day of the wedding. And it was heavy. I used two, three Kotex every hour. My mom wouldn't let me wear tampons. Mexican mothers are like that. And the *crinolina* that I had underneath my wedding dress, it was all stained. Between my legs, it was messy. All streaked. And then after the wedding, we had to do that *Pinche Dinero*.

"*Pinche Dinero*?" Gwen asked.

"It's a dance, where everyone dances with the bride and pins a dollar on her dress. Mine was a five-dollar *Pinche Dinero*. When I went to change, I just left the dress there with all the money on it. It was all dirty. All brown. And then when we went for the honeymoon, I had changed into pants. And when we got out of the car, my husband said to me, 'You're stained.' I yelled at him. 'Who are you to tell me that?' And when we got inside the hotel, I locked myself in the bathroom and cried and cried. And in the morning, the bed was stained again. I came back from my honeymoon *intacto*. The same way I left."

Intacto, Janice thought. *The same way I left.*

Assigned to a cell, Janice crouched over the toilet and retched. Someone (her sleeping cellmate, it had to be) had taped a Bible bookmark over the toilet:

> *Behold the birds of the heaven, that they sow not, neither do they reap, nor gather into barns; and your heavenly Father feedeth them. Are not ye of much more value then they?*

Yes, God, Janice said, curling on cement. I am worth more than a bird, and I wish that you would sometime *act like it*. God, who so loved the world, where dreams shriveled at an astounding rate, flash stop photography fast-forwarding a flower's death. God, who promises not to keep you safe, Sr. Gloria said, but to never leave you. *My God, my God, why have you forsaken me?*

Even Jesus said it.

God is the god of the present, Sr. Gloria said. *If you stay in the present, God is with you.*

Fuck that also, Janice thought. When had the present moment ever been good? Okay, maybe here and there. Squatting on a curb sharing a cigarette, arms wrapping her after sex, the warm buzzing alcohol plateau before sobs wracked her body. Fleeting, all. The goddamn morning always came. The sun returned, blasphemous in its consistency, making her look really shitty in five-dollar makeup.

Janice curled her body around the stabbing ache in her side.

For I have been in the belly of the whale.

Her cellmate sat up in bed, looking dazed. She was a stop sign-shaped blonde in her mid-fifties with a drug-ravaged face.

"Who are you?"

"Zelda of the Night."

"Well." The woman ruffled the back of her hair. "Glad to have the company. Most of these bitches don't talk. The dying art of conversation!"

"SHUT UP!" A voice across the cellblock shouted.

"You want to sit on the bed?" She patted the scratchy gray military blanket. "We'll chat?"

"I'm cool here," Janice said, pressing her face against the metal toilet seat.

"You're probably wondering what I'm in for." The woman regarded her coyly. "I did something artistic. Something *bad*."

Janice vomited violently.

"Oh, Sweetie."

Janice wiped strings of mucus and bile from her face.

"You know that skinny bitch won't let you in the sick bay. You got to ask the night guard. The one with the prosthetic foot."

Janice wiped her face on her shirt.

"Right, my story. Like I was saying, this *yoga* studio moved into my neighborhood. And my boyfriend, he was ogling the girls when they came out. He would talk about their 'yoga bodies.' But I was like, yoga? No, I'm on a fixed income. So I went to the studio and said, "I'll take the ten classes for ten dollars." And the owner said, "Lady, I can smell alcohol on your breath." And I was like, "That is not possible, as I am wearing cologne." And he was like, "Ma'am, please leave the premises." And the next week, he installed this dark glass in the windows, so I couldn't even peek in."

"SHUT UP!" the voice down the cell block yelled.

"So I was like: okay, very rude and hurtful. And, being an artist—I was a middle school art teacher—that night I took a can of spray paint and made that glass my canvas. Modern art!"

"What did you paint?" Janice asked.

"Yoga boners, mostly. Plus some choice words for that—

"SHUT UP OR I WILL STICK A BROOM HANDLE SO FAR UP YOUR CUNT IT'LL COME OUT YOUR EYE!" the voice down the cellblock shouted.

"Guess those are the rapists," Janice said.

"Oh, no," the cellmate said. "That's just Tabitha."

For I have been in the belly of the whale.
And I came out of there intacto. The same way I left.

Except you don't come out intact, Janice thought, curled on cold cement. You come out stinking like fish. You get vomited onto the sand. Rot in the sun. Gulls tear at your flesh. Sand flies jump from your decaying skin.

Nausea rising.

There is nothing left, Janice pleaded. There is nothing left.

Janice shielded her eyes.

"So this is me hitting rock bottom?"

"More or less," the angel said.

"It feels like shit."

"Yes," the angel said.

"Please intervene."

"Yes."

"Now would be a good time."

The angel put its hand on Janice's head.

"Thank you," Janice said.

The angel heaved Janice over its shoulder, and limped down the hallway.

✵ VIRTUE OF THE MONTH ✵

I know she drank her coffee black. I know she had high cheekbones and copper hair. I know she suffered from migraine headaches, that she was diagnosed as manic-depressive, that she received electro-shock therapy.

This is my mother, Olivia Freedman. She hung herself from a rafter when I was four years old.

"I'm getting a headache," I tell Ben. I am curled against the warm window of the passenger side of his truck, knees drawn to chest.

Ben turns the radio down. We are on the fourth hour of this five-hour drive to my father's house. Ben has been singing along with the rock station, church choir tenor mingling with crackling static.

I look past his profile, at the small town traffic, the spindly palm trees whipping in the wind. Hot car exhaust mingles with the smell of gasoline and the fried, oily odor of Luby's Cafeteria-Restaurant. The sign on the buffet place has removable black letters, like a movie theater marquee. *Luby's for lent!* The sign declares. *Tilapia! Catfish! Salmon Filet!*

We roll past peeling storefronts, black iron benches, a small church. On its well-kept lawn, a sign: *Virtud de Mes: Honestidad.* "The virtue of the month is honesty," I inform Ben.

"Then tell me," he says. "What's the craziest thing you've ever done?"

A thread of images blurs my mind. Bleak and terrifying, all.

"When I was in college, I would go swimming in the fountains. By myself. In the middle of the night."

"Maybe you were a dolphin in a past life."

"I see myself as more of a hermit crab."

"Maybe we were hermit crabs together."

"In a past life? No way. You would have been a dolphin."

My mother wore dresses sewn from floursack, dresses worn until they were worn out, worn-out dresses cut to aprons, quilt squares, rags. She was sixteen in the humid Texarkana summer, canning tomatoes while her parents were in town. Water boiled on all the burners, jars sucked in their seals, water steamed up, boiled down. Olivia tried not to drop hot jars, tried not to burn her fingers, tried not to spoil the fruit. She sent her youngest brother—an epileptic—to fetch water from the open well.

He was eight years old.

He had a seizure, fell in.

Drowned.

Day two in Plano. My father's sunken living room is carpeted with ochre shag, yarn I yanked at as a child. I sit down at the piano, plunk some stale notes.

"I didn't know you played." Ben peels off his paint-flecked work shirt, flops on the couch.

"Sweetheart." I spin around on the piano bench. "Chopsticks doesn't count." Ben pulls a *National Geographic* from the coffee table, flips it open. His face is eager, searching, bright.

I don't know where he came from. Darkness rolls off him like water, the weight of the world does not grate him down. His face lights up at my voice, the mention of dinner, the prospect of sex.

"I'd kill for your endorphins," I say.

"If you want endorphins, go on a run."

"Ben. What's the worst thing that's ever happened to you?"

"In high school, I had tonsillitis so bad my throat closed up." His dimples fade. "I could only eat yogurt for a month."

My laughter comes out hard and brittle. Frightening.

"Jesus, Laura. I lost, like, thirty pounds."

"Oh my God." I rub my face with my hands. "Want to know the worst thing that ever happened to me?"

He braces himself.

I flop on top of him, burrow my face in his neck. "My boyfriend tried to make me go running."

He swats me with the magazine. "It would actually be good for you."

Thanks for doing this," I say, trying my teeth on his collarbone. "Thanks for coming with me."

"Baby." Ben stretches and yawns. "I'm getting paid."

It's true—my lawyer brother is paying us to spend a weekend preparing the house for sale. It's sat empty, gathering dust, since our father died six months back. I'm sorting photos and letters, folding clothes into boxes. Ben is painting over the peeling yellow with a tasteful tan. He is eager to supplement his income with odd jobs, subsisting, as he currently is, on parental largesse and student loans. When he finishes his MBA in June, however, he will plunge with alacrity into the world of energy consulting and economics.

"You're my favorite sellout," I whisper, and kiss him on the temple.

Olivia's mother was a grim-lipped woman, hair tightly wound. She blamed Olivia for her brother's death, radiating silent coldness, accusation wearing wrinkles in her face. Olivia left home at eighteen, lived in a boarding house, worked as a secretary. She met my father while waiting in line for peanuts at the movies.

Ten years later, Olivia was in a tract home in Plano, with two kids and her auto mechanic husband. She got word that her mother was on her deathbed, waiting to see her daughter, wanting to make peace.

Olivia got a migraine. She stayed in her room for three days, until word came: her mother had died.

I stand in the garden, watering grapefruit. Ben walks along the roof, agile and balanced, lengthening shadow echoing steps.

Standing in this garden, my mother felt a fog steam and darken her brain. Dingy loudness. Rustling like wings of sparrows.

I look at Ben, with the sunset boiling through his leather tool belt and wavy hair. I shift the stream of water towards the pomegranate tree, where unripe fruit hang stunted by frost, tiny and green.

Standing in this garden, my mother felt a fog steam and darken her brain. Agitation rose in her flesh—a feeling of fish biting her skin, water receding beneath her, a vacuum opening outward into time.

Some mornings, riled with anger, Olivia would unmake beds, stuff sheets in the washer, vacuum violently, scream at those who crossed her path. Some mornings, she gardened, whistled, let me crack eggs in a bowl and roll round mounds of snicker doodle dough. She drank, and hid beer cans behind the sewing machine. She made a scene in church. Slit her wrists in the bathtub. Inhaled chemicals in a toilet bowl. She came back from the hospital, passive and dazed. She played Euchre. She dieted. In photographs, she was pleasant, loving, laughing. Beautiful.

Ben stands behind me, drinking lemonade. Examining photographs I've laid out like solitaire cards on the table.

He taps the edge of a picture. "You look like her." In the snapshot, Olivia holds a hard-shelled suitcase in a shipyard, her floral shirt tucked into a woolen skirt. Behind her, a car hangs suspended by a crane. She is laughing, wearing lipstick.

"She doesn't look crazy." Ben frowns.

"Sometimes she was normal. Sometimes she was fine."

After six months of dating, Ben still believes that my Seroquel tablets are for epilepsy; that my shrink visits are weekly massages. I guess I seemed stable when I met him. At twenty-six, I have suede suit jackets, potted cacti on my porch, and a job teaching English to migrant farmworkers. I read more books in a month than Ben does in a year.

And this is my longest-running relationship. Other boyfriends left when I emphasized a point by throwing a bowl of salad out the window, or slapped them in the face for crunching too loudly on saltines. But my meds are better adjusted now. And Ben is more accepting, or less observant, than any other man I've loved.

In my father's closet, I find a ledger book. In the front is a record of my father's stocks. In the back, terse notations regarding my mother's episodes:

April 3rd: *3 bottles behind the radiator.*

April 7th: *O. dropped kids at Sunday school, stopped at the liquor store, bought wine. Confrontation in the parking lot.*

April 10th: *Came home from work, found her in bed, cuddling with the baby. Drunk. Liquor on her breath.*

We sleep in my father's bed. A red and brown quilt, pillows that smell like dust. I lie unsleeping in the house where migraines came to my mother, pressed in on her, crushed her until she could not breathe. The air is close and tight. The force of gravity growing. I unfold myself from Ben's arms; get up to open a window. But there are no windows in this bedroom. I stand by the bed. I stare at the wall. It is puckered with textured stucco, prickly beneath paint.

"What are you doing?" Ben asks, eyes half open. He lifts the covers with one arm.

I climb back in bed, rest my head on his chest. Spooned against the warm curl of his body, fumigation takes place. Damp toads sleeping in the cave of my chest awaken. One by one, they hop away.

Dream: The Bureaucracy of Heaven

File Clerk: No suicides.

Olivia: (*Crazed silence.*)

Me: You've got to consider her circumstances.

File Clerk: (*Lifting a stack of papers.*) Despair is the greatest sin. (*Raises eyebrows.*) The sin of Judas.

Me: Judas betrayed *Jesus*. (*Taking Olivia by the arm.*) Surely one suicide does not compare.

File Clerk: (*Glances at records.*) Peter betrayed Jesus when the cock crowed three times. Yet he stands at the gate of heaven. Judas went to hell for hanging himself in the potter's field.

Me: (*Incredulity.*)

File Clerk: Despair is the greatest sin. (*Thumbs through regulations.*) The failure to believe God's redemptive power. Suicide is a sin of despair.

Me: Then I feel sorry for Judas.

File clerk: (*Raises eyebrows, lowers glasses on nose.*) Dante made suicides into bleeding trees.

Me: (*To Olivia*) Let's go.

The next morning, I sit on the garage steps. A pink and hoary scrub brush rests beside me, a disheveled but obedient pet. My father used it to scrape duck shit from my shoes, after they'd yanked stale bread from our hands. I'd stood on the cement picnic table, surrounded by toothless beaks. Afraid.

I open my notebook. Write her a note.

Olivia:

> *This is the logic of suicide:*
> *(£) Suffering > (Ω) Coping Mechanisms = (∞) Unbearable Suffering*
> *Given: Death (Θ) = cessation of suffering*
> *Answer: Death (Θ)*
> *See, but what if you reduced (£) or increased (Ω)? Then:*
> *(£)Suffering < (Ω) Coping Mechanisms = (Ψ) Bearable Suffering*

Dust motes swim below the rafters. The window gleams, piercing and bright. My eyes unfocus, and Olivia appears—filmy, electric blue, muttering to herself.

I put the rope around my neck, thin and scratchy. Then I saw it, flashing, how it would happen, white clatter of light going out in my brain.

"Mom," I say, cheeks wet.

The walls assault me with their whiteness, these curtains hang at my neck like vines, I clutch at the drapes and pull them, get me out of this house.

"It's me."

Olivia looks into my eyes. She is suddenly chewing on a cigarette. Sitting next to me on the step. Calm. Exhausted.

This happens to you too, you know. She touches my cheek. *Don't worry, babe.* Her hand is soft, and strangely warm. *You've got a good year left.* She flickers, then shorts out.

Ben finds me sitting on the garage steps. He eases down beside me, bad knee cracking.

I poke at a fissure in the cement. "This house creeps me out."

Ben surveys a wastebasket of hoary tennis balls, orderly rows of tinned meat, mop heads fraying with grime. He tucks his hair behind his ears. "I found something in the crawlspace."

Ben has found a bamboo picnic basket filled with my mother's papers, wedged between fragile oriental plates and ancient barbell hand weights. We repair to the living room, and finger through a sheaf of onionskin documents. At the top: "*English 103. Olivia Freedman.*" Twelve essays from a community college English course.

"*A Memorable Day*" details a visit to the circus with my brother and me. "*Never having seen an elephant in the flesh, I wondered if the great gray creature would inspire the sense of wonder I have read of in books. I was not* disappointed. *The clown's antics delighted Stephen, and I could not help but join in his laughter. Laura, however, was frightened by the shouting and clanging, so I fed her with peppermints . . ."*

"*The Most Interesting Person I Know*" offers a description of me at three years old. "*While Stephen was at his first day of school this fall, I had busied myself in the kitchen, cutting the crusts from Laura's sandwiches. When I called Laura to the table, she was nowhere to be found. Fearing she had wandered away, I searched up and down the street. I finally found her a block from the school, cuddling her kitten. She said that Mischief wanted to learn the alphabet, too.*"

"This isn't right." I hand Ben "*My Favorite Object,*" "*An Oriental Wedding,*" and "*My Recipe for Cheese Biscuits.*" "She sounds like June Cleaver."

"What did you expect? *I Hurt Myself Today to See If I Still Feel?*"

"It's phony. It's not *her.*"

"You were four when she died." He sets his hand on my knee. "How would you possibly know?"

"Trust me, I know."

"She's not *you*, Laura."

Hairs prickle on my neck. "What's that supposed to mean?"

"You're mad her essays aren't like pages from your diary."

"My *diary*?"

"You left it open on the dresser, Laura. It was an invitation."

"I trusted you!"

"Not enough to tell me you take anti-psychotic medication."

"They're mood stabilizers!"

"Well they're not working very well, are they?"

I take a deep breath.

Center myself. Then slap him. "Get out."

"Gladly."

He grabs his keys and his jacket. The door slams shut.

In the bedroom, I flip open my journal, rereading what I've written, what he's read.

March 5th—*Another pimple on my cheek. I've counted seven. It looks like someone ordered a pizza to my face.*

March 6th—*I unraveled. See? This morning. I came apart like paper in water, I ripped up, I shredded, I want out of this body, I am afraid of this face. I want to tear off these dresses, take them off, I can't be here, I can't be here.*

March 7th—*Life has always been pretty hard farming, and at this point, I kind of just want it to be over.*

March 8th—*Dr. T. upped the Lithium. I don't feel a fucking thing.*

March 9th—*Marcie asked me what it was like to date Ben. I told her it was like adopting a golden retriever.*

March 10th—*He is the puppy, I am the bitch.*

I run hot water in the pale yellow bathtub, peel off my rings and bracelets, unfurl my hair from its clumsily wadded bun. Rising steam fogs the mirror, erasing mascara streaks and swollen eyes. The water scalds my hand, but I step in anyway, no slip flowers on the tub's base sandpapery against my heels. Tight streaks of muscle unclench in my back. I soak. Olivia tried it here, cooking herself before cutting herself. Warm water running to blood. A stretch, a tear. Death like a birth. My toes bob out of the water. Breathe air. The crackle of static softens to snow.

I pull on a tank top and borrow the bottom half of my father's gray sweat suit. He wore it as he bent to peel up sand dollars in the wind, brushing off silt with dry thumbs. The lamp on the piano has a hollow base of glass, filled with coral and sea urchin shells. It illuminates the living room as I kneel to gather my mother's papers, replace them in their box. Take them out to the garage.

Olivia is in there, doing laundry, chewing on a bobby pin. *Takes a lot of bleach to get blood out of blankets.* She kicks the washing machine with her slipper. *Take it from me. When you slit your wrists, stay in the tub.*

I recognize the fabric she's loading—the swatches that make up my bedroom quilt. But instead of scraps, they are blouses and dresses. Whole.

"Listen," I say, setting the box down. "I don't blame you for what you did. But maybe I have a little more self-control."

Oh yes. She takes my chin in her hand. *You're the queen of self-control.*

"That doesn't mean I'll make the same choice."

She studies my face. *I wish you wouldn't wear my costume jewelry like its real jewelry.*

I touch my earrings. "I got these at a craft fair."

It's not a choice.

"Are you saying there's no free will?"

Free will was when I chose between eggs and oatmeal. Lolling her head to the side, she mimes hanging herself. *That wasn't a choice.*

"If it wasn't a choice, it wasn't a sin. And if it wasn't a sin, you should be in heaven. Or, Jesus, I don't know! Purgatory, at least."

You'll have to pass that on to the authorities.

"What are you doing in the garage?"

She looks at me. *This is my heaven. Doing laundry for eternity. Being insulted by my little girl.* She throws her hands in the air. *Hallelujah. Glory be!*

And then she is gone.

Breathing mold spores in the dark, I listen for Ben. My hair is a tangle of wet snakes on the pillow. The radiator cooks dust, humming with heat. Finally: a fumbling at the front door, keys clanking to the counter. Ben runs water in the kitchen, opens the fridge. *The bedroom the bedroom the bedroom,* I will him. *Don't sleep on the couch.*

"Hey," he says. He is standing in the doorway, backlit by the bathroom light.

"Hey." I pat the scratchy comforter.

Steadying himself with the doorframe, bracing one foot against the other in turn, he steps out of his sneakers. He flops on the bed, smelling like paint flecks and deodorant and crushed leaves.

I pick a piece of lint from my sweat pants. "Sorry I smacked you."

"Eh. You're not that strong."

I hold my toes, cold outside the covers. "You shouldn't have read my diary."

"You shouldn't have lied to me."

I point to myself. "Sin of omission." I point to him. "Sin of commission."

"Technicalities. What matters is that we can trust each other."

"I have a lot of baggage."

"Everyone has baggage."

"Mine's heavier."

He rubs my back, trailing his hand between my shoulder blades. "You know, you also wrote about how much you like me."

"Yeah?"

"Yeah. Pages and pages. It was really sweet."

Ben and I look at each other across the pillow. I expect to see something in those dark pools—some secret, some answer. But I just see his eyes, soft and moist. A creature unafraid of scrutiny because he hasn't been hurt.

"You know what the thing about my mom is? The thing that scares me?"

"Huh?"

"I don't think it was a choice."

Ben touches my hair. "You always have a choice."

"I don't want my story to end like that."

"It won't."

"I'm not sure I believe that."

"What can I do?"

"To what?"

"To make you believe it?"

I shut my eyes, and doorway light blurs the blackness. Rising from the carpet: the smell of damp towels and broken sand dollars. Ben's fingers trace the side of my face, fingering my earrings, stroking the tiny wisps of fur along my earlobes.

I blink, a cavern of birds opening in my stomach.

"I don't know."

✷ ELEPHANTS NEVER FORGET ✷

FROM: janiceaureliagibbs@honeylocusttech.edu
TO: splunkmiester@splunkspace.com
DATE: Wednesday, April 23, at 10:35PM
SUBJECT: Your Book!!!

Dear Cody,

I was in the bookstore getting bored with my medical terminology flashcards, kicking myself for buying a rip-off $3.00 iced coffee that took 3 seconds to drink, when I saw this guy reading a book titled *Elephants Never Forget.* The cover featured an orange elephant silhouette against an ivory background. I squinted at the author's name: Cody Splunk. I spit my coffee out. I did. I literally *spit* it. I was like, "Dude, my friend wrote that book!" The guy looked at me like I was crazy and pointed to an ENTIRE STACK of *Elephants Never Forget.* Cody! There are, like, 5 copies of your book sitting there, which indicates that people are buying them, and possibly even reading them. That is so cool! You must be, like, rolling around on your bed in a gigantic pile of cash. I've only gotten through the first chapter so far, but I like what you are doing with the futuristic dystopia where exotic wildlife are extinct and people believe that elephants are mystical creatures. I don't know why GovCo, the sinister government-corporation hybrid kidnapped the protagonist's girlfriend, but I'm sure Clint McClintock and his ruggedly handsome face will get to the bottom of the conspiracy. Nice author photo, by the way. Where'd you get the horse?

Update on me: I ditched Texas for the brave new world of Kentucky. Piggott, Kentucky to be precise. What? You haven't heard of Piggott, Kentucky? Don't worry, no one has. It is, however, the jam capital of Kentucky. It also boasts a museum with over 300 wax figures depicting the Old and New Testament. The museum also has two rooms of Christian martyrs, and Kentucky's largest Braille Bible.

I'm living with my Dad and Stepmom, which actually isn't bad. In Texas I had, like, a weekly screaming match with Glenda. Once I threw a cat at her. But now we enjoy secretly smoking cigarettes on the porch. I'm working on my Radiology Tech degree, and I've got a work-study job at the Student Success Center. I must say that I am a fan of the desk job. I pretty much sit here, do my homework, and occasionally tell people to sign the binder. But when I graduate with my degree, I can make up to, like, $52,000 a year! Then it will be me rolling around on a pile of cash! Yahahahaha!

Anyway, my boss is due back from her lunch break, so I should pretend to be working. Write back if you have a minute! I'd love to know what's new with you, Mr. "I-had-a-write-up-in-*The Rio Grande Star*-and-neglected-to-tell-my-old-friend."

Stay cool,
Janice

FROM: splunkmeister@spunkspace.com
TO: janiceaureliagibbs@honeylocusttech.edu
DATE: Thursday, April 24, at 9:32AM
SUBJECT: RE: Your Book!

Dear Janice,

SO GREAT TO HEAR FROM YOU!!! I've been responding to all of this fan mail asking boneheaded questions like, "So how did elephant DNA get written into Clint McClintock's DNA in the first place? And it's like, did you even read past page 300, sir? I waste hours responding to such queries, when I should really be working on my sequel, *Elephants Never Forget II: Elephant Burial Grounds.* Anyway, it was amazing to open the 99th e-mail with the subject line "Your Book!" and find a miracle: Janice Gibbs.

It sounds like you have all your marbles in one sock, as my grandma says. Radiology Tech is a good degree. My sister was thinking about going for that, but instead she decided to go for sitting in front of the TV drinking microwaved ice cream. When my book came out, everyone in the family quit their jobs, so finances are actually kind of tight! Nonetheless, it is amazing to buy the things we've always needed, like Tory's asthma meds and Greebo's Hummer dealership.

I am actually doing a reading in Lexington in May (crazy coincidence!). I looked it up and it's only two and a half hours from Piggott. I can make the drive in my rental car, *no problem*, if you feel like having lunch. I'll have my assistant call you. Kidding! (I don't have an assistant! But sometimes Tory pretends to be my assistant on the phone, and then people are like, "Why does your assistant make those weird growling noises?") Anyways, let me know if you're up for it. It would make my decade!

Your friend,
Cody

FROM: janiceaureliagibbs@honeylocusttech.edu
TO: splunkmeister@splunkspace.com
DATE: Sunday, May 25, at 2:38AM
SUBJECT: blast from the past

Hey Splunkmeister—

When you set off the alarm in the wax museum, I had a flashback to sneaking around *Bridges*. Sigh. Those were the days. Actually, though, they kind of weren't. I'm way happier now. Sorry there was gravel in your burger. Small town—not too many dining options.

It was hard for me to answer your question about why I finally left the Valley. To elaborate: After my brush with the law, I was in this halfway house, eating expired egg salad, getting my underwear stolen. The duffel bag of stuff I scavenged from my aunt's rampage included one reading item: Ms. Freedman's diary. So lying under a moth-eaten blanket, too depressed to move, I took up and read. The stroll down memory lane inspired me to contemplate the awful fates of our homeroom frenemies.

1) Julie Chang: Got a traumatic brain injury in Iraq.

2) Kristi Colimote: Drank a bottle of Lysol to get attention from her boyfriend. When he found her 3 days later, her left side was dead and her kidneys were shot. (He did not stick around to help her with the catheter.)

3) Phil Gasher: Got hit over the head with a tube sock of combination locks at Huntsville State Penitentiary.

And I was like, okay, Ms. Freedman, you failed. Why couldn't you have been the teacher from one of those movies where a nice lady with good bone structure stands on her desk and reads a poem and the kids are all like, fuck poverty, we're going to college!

Lying there under the scratchy blanket, I was feeling how hopeless it is to try to help or save people, because their lives keep going forward like trains on a track, moving toward the gaping maw grinding jaw of evil fate. Then I got to the part of the journal where Ms. Freedman gets batshit crazy/biblical: "*Isaiah 45:9: The clay does not ask the potter: what are you making?*"

Meaning: we are clay, God's taking pottery 101. Meaning: ain't our place asking God why she keeps mashing our faces in. We may think the ashtray is getting ruined, but, surprise! God is really making us into gorgeous Precious Moments figurines.

I find this problematic because for one, Precious Moments are creepy. Two: in this halfway house, the saying "God don't make mistakes" gets bandied about like a favorite beach ball. Sherrie says, "I feel bad that I was a meth-whore and CPS took my eleven kids," and Amber says, "That's okay, Sherrie, God don't make mistakes."

But it wasn't God who made Sherrie the blowjob queen of the I-80 underpass. She did that to herself! Yes, Sherrie got molested by her uncle and abused by her husband and the sciatica made it hard for her to keep that factory job, but God didn't light that first bowl under her then-existent teeth.

I have the same problem with the "The clay does not ask the potter 'what are you making?'" thing. Because, honestly: I do not think God made me into a broke homeless pill-popping thief. Some bad shit happened to me, yes. But God didn't hold a lightning bolt to my head and say: "Janice A. Gibbs, you swallow Shirley's Diazepam. Take a fifty from the cash drawer. Keep fucking up your life so I can make you into a useless ceramic ashtray." Even now, if I wanted to, I could swallow my pride, call Glenda, and say, "Wire me money for a bus ride to Piggot. I'm coming home."

Then I realized: I should just fucking do that.

So I did.

Good luck with the Rags2Riches shoot. I'm sure it will get you a lot of publicity, but it seems like the host chick is all about the drama. She's always trying to reunite "Riches" with, like, childhood bullies from when they were "Rags." I've seen, like, fifteen slap fights on that show. So. Be warned.

Love,

J.

[Transcript of TeenTV's *Rags2Riches*]

(Wide shot of CODY SPLUNK on horseback in JANICE'S front yard. Cut to HARPER.)

HARPER: This Riches is getting ready for his horseback proposal. Cody, are you feeling the butterflies?

CODY: Uh, yeah.

HARPER: I'm ringing the door for you, okay? *(Rings bell.)*

JANICE: *(Opens door.)*

HARPER: I'm Harper, and this is RAGS 2 RICHES.

JANICE: Dear God. *(Clutches forehead.)*

HARPER: Do you remember Cody Splunk?

JANICE: *(irritably)* I had lunch with him last week.

HARPER: He's gone from RAGS . . . to RICHES! *(HARPER steps back.)*

CODY: *(Horse clops into view.)* Janice Gibbs. *(Proffers ring.)* Will you marry me?

JANICE: What?

HARPER: The nerd is getting with the Goth girl, peoples! This is so freaking sweet!

JANICE: Oh my God. Cody. Get off the horse.

HARPER: This was his idea, angel-face.

CODY: *(Looking unsure.)* What sayest thou, my lady Janice? Your white horse awaits ye.

HARPER: That's a forty- carat diamond, girl. I'd put that on if I were you.

JANICE: Listen, shut that off.

HARPER: *(Pointing at Janice.)* My cameras do what they want.

JANICE: I will bite off your finger, so help me God.

HARPER: He's already turned it off. No need to be so sensitive.

JANICE: Cody. What were you thinking?

CODY: That I love you.

JANICE: *(Shaking head.)* You can't.

CODY: But I do.

JANICE: You can't just, have a lunch date and then ask me to marry you a week later. It doesn't work like that.

CODY: *(Closes helmet visor. Spurs horse. Horse trots a few feet, then chews on gladiolas.)*

HARPER: There he goes, peoples! Galloping into the distance!

JANICE: I thought you said that thing was off.

HARPER: Janice, tell the viewers why you shot this Riches down.

JANICE: You are a TERRIBLE PERSON.

HARPER: You're the one who broke his heart, doll.

JANICE: *(Slams door.)*

FROM: janiceaureliagibbs@honeylocusttech.edu
TO: splunkmeister@splunkspace.com
DATE: Friday, June 13, at 7:58PM
SUBJECT: Train Wreck

Cody:

They're still out there stomping on the gladiolas. Glenda was going to give that skank the back end of her frying pan but I told her we should just call the cops. I am *so sorry* for that fiasco. Those people are using your emotions in a desperate bid for ratings. Don't sign *anything* they give you.

As for the proposal: you can't love me, Cody. You don't know me. I barely know myself.

Let me know if you're still up for being friends.

Always,
Janice

FROM: janiceaureliagibbs@honeylocusttech.edu
TO: splunkmeister@splunkspace.com
DATE: Sunday, September 7, at 2:31PM
SUBJECT: Ms. Freedman's wedding

Dear Cody,

I was wondering if you are going or not. I want to go but I feel like it will be awkward if I don't know anyone. You know my number.

J.

P.S. I'm halfway through *Elephants Never Forget II: Elephant Burial Grounds*. Not bad, Splunk.

FROM: laura@uncommonhappiness.com
TO: janiceaureliagibbs@honeylocusttech.edu
DATE: Monday, February 9, at 10:54AM
SUBJECT: thank you

Dear Janice,

Thank you for the goose and gander bride and groom salt and pepper shakers, and thank you for coming out for my special day. I was sorry Cody couldn't make it. He said he had a reading in Chicago, but I think he's still frazzled from that TeenChannel fiasco—I know I am. They interviewed me for two hours, then cut it to the five minutes where I talked about his cape fetish. I still feel bad about that.

In other news: we are pregnant! That is, I am pregnant. Three months along. I am undergoing the complex process of tapering off meds, as they could damage the baby. Something of a roller coaster! Let me know if you have any stellar name suggestions. We are compiling a list, to which Ben keeps adding candidates like "Treader" and "Sport." I am hoping to go with something more traditional, like "Diane" or "Rose."

Congratulations on making the honor roll! Knowing that you are doing so well is the best present you could ever give me.

Love,
Ms. Freedman

✳ UNCOMMON HAPPINESS ✳

The purpose of psychiatry, according to Sigmund Freud, is to bring patients from "hysteric misery to common unhappiness." This is a forum for the emotionally labile (and we are many) who instead seek "uncommon happiness," a well-being brought into sharper relief by the darkness we've fled.

Hola Readers,

So, maybe you (like me) make your living doing something you're not super proud of (say, admission essay consulting for the progeny of uber-rich helicopter parents) and it kind of makes you feel like hamsters are eating your soul. But maybe you (like me) have discussed this with a therapist and agreed it is a necessary sacrifice, considering you work two hours a day, which leaves your high maintenance face time for isometric aerobics and journaling about your empty, empty, heart. And while you could take the city bus downtown and tutor poor kids for $10/hour, this would not enable you to buy your very expensive meds, which you need in order to keep noticing the beautiful and the good (like the glint of mica in the gravel as the car hum tapers off; the moment to breathe beneath the aching tree limbs before you fold your soul into a box and go inside to re-write an entitled 17-year-old's admission essay to Duke).

Just as, say, a hypothetical example.

Then this is the website for you.

I just sat down with a glass of milk and a jar of peanut butter (you get to do these things when pregnant) to answer your questions. Let's get to it!

Dear Laura,

Like bears, my boyfriend and I snuggle all day. We nuzzle each other's faces, drifting in and out of naps. I used to wake up at five, run 11 miles, and do 100 squats. Now that I have Jasper, though, I just want to snuggle and eat cheese. Sometimes I worry that the oxytocin is clouding my brain, making me stupid and sleepy. But it wasn't exactly ambition that drove me when I was more proactive about perfecting my body. It was crushing sadness. So I decided that the fact that Jasper and I spend all weekend sleeping and cuddling means the birds pecking at my brain are gone.

Then I got a bedsore.

What now?

~*Type A in Omaha*

Dear Type A,

The real question here (bedsore aside) is one of complacency vs. contentment. Complacency means sinking into oblivion: ignoring our country's unjust infrastructure and moral stagnation. The compulsive running indicates complacency is not your problem. Contentment, on the other elbow, means . . . well, I don't know. I'm not very good at it. Like you, I'm attuned to what's wrong. Take me out to a restaurant, and I'll fixate on the waitress's sad eyes and the unethically sourced shrimp. I'll come home reeling with *weltshmerz*, and stay up until 3 A.M. making online donations to UNICEF.

I'm a party and a half.

It seems that Jasper helps you with that whole "learning to relax and enjoy life" project—this makes him a keeper in my book. But maybe Jasper could join you in a few fitness activities, thus eliminating the looming bedsore threat.

Dear Laura,

I love your column in the *Living* section, and I've followed your blog since its inception. Here's my situation: Having identified my sex life as an untapped spring of happiness, I asked my husband to consider roleplay. He filled jam

jars with sexy "roles" and steamy "locations." I was excited to give it a go—
until I reached in the jar and pulled out "Lifeguard/Beached Whale," and
"Schoolteacher/Bag of Circus Peanuts."

"You're not taking this seriously!" I cried, throwing a handful of paper slips.

"Since when is sex serious?" he asked.

I'm at a real loss here, Laura. How do I make love to a bag of circus peanuts?

~Beached Whale in Trenton

Dear Trenton,

You made yourself vulnerable by suggesting roleplay. Your husband failed to
meet you at that place of soul-baring exchange. Maybe he's not comfortable
sharing his true fantasies. Or maybe he just can't resist a good punchline.
Whatever the root of his humor-based cop out, discussion is imperative.
Choose a quiet time in a private location, such as a breakfast nook, or a car.
Once, I took advantage of a 10-hour drive to Mexico to address my husband's
passive-aggressive gargling. This created a "safe space" for him to observe that
I'd been flushing my meds down the toilet. By the time we reached Matamoros,
we shared a new emotional intimacy along with our platter of street tacos.

So, Trenton: muster your best non-accusatory tone, and share how the
circus-peanut experience made you feel. Hopefully, he'll open up as well.

Dear Laura,

I think you misunderstood my question. What I meant was: how do I treat
a bedsore? Wash it? Use antibiotic cream?

~Type A in Omaha

Dear Type A,

This is not a medical website. Please consult a doctor.

Dear Laura,

I have Spinal Muscular Atrophy type three. At best I'll live to twenty-five.
Before then, my arms will wither into pointy chicken bones. I'll lose the

ability to clasp a pencil, to swallow, to breathe. I'm fifteen, and I've already been in the wheelchair for a year.

It's going to be a rough decade.

When I read *Glamour*, I feel like shit. When I see dancing, I claw at my palms in jealousy. When I read a novel, I would trade the rest of my life for one day in a slightly more functional suit of skin: one that would graciously permit me to run across a moor. Fall backwards into a fountain. Get on a bus without a goddamn ordeal.

How do I keep believing that my life has value?

~Lucy in San Francisco

Dear Lucy:

Our culture says your value lies in how you look and what you produce. But our culture is—and this is apparent when you page through *Glamour*—sort of vapid. For my first six months out of the nut ward, I heard the whispering of "you're worthless" every day. I had to fight to believe that my infinitesimal actions (because really, I hardly moved) made a ripple in the struggle for a more humane and less shitty world. Now that I serve acceptable societal functions (I'm married, pregnant, earning fat cashwads) I still struggle against a current of self-recrimination (*Instead of accompanying the poor in their struggle for justice, Laura, you maintain the hegemony of the rich by polishing their Harvard applications.*)

It helps to surround yourself with words and people who affirm your faith that the heart is more important than the body, that what you do is not who you are. You might consider keeping a web journal of your struggle. If you look into it, let me know—I'll post a link.

Dear Laura,

Primitive skills—the survival techniques of native cultures—are my husband's obsession. During his lunch hour, Tim reads about tracking, scouting, foraging, and tanning. Every evening, he plays Indian in our backyard. He cuts sapling branches, strips them of bark, bends them to bows. He smashes bottles, and chips shards to form fine points. He digs clay from creeks, shapes pots, and paints them with fine powder ground from red rock. He peels out the fibrous interior of dry stinging nettle vines, and twists them into cordage. Yesterday, he ate a grasshopper.

I'm not very outdoorsy. Can this marriage be saved?

~*Indoorsy in Indianapolis*

Dear Indoorsy,

It all depends on how comfortable you and your husband are with each other's predilections. If he respects your indoorsiness, and you appreciate his grasshopper-eating skills, I don't see a problem.

Dear Laura,

I made some iced tea, sat Darrel down on the porch. "Honey," I said. "When you mocked my interest in role play, I felt rejected."

"I wasn't mocking."

"Zookeeper/Underage Orangutan? Sexy Venus Flytrap/Pound of Horse meat?"

"Honey, when I imagine you're an underage orangutan, I get rock hard." I glanced at his shorts.

He wasn't lying.

We had the best sex of our marriage this afternoon. I just thought you should know!

~*Beached (and glowing)*
Whale in Trenton

Dear Trenton,

Maybe that's what love is: embracing your partner at his place of deepest strangeness. After all, I accept that my husband reads *The Wall Street Journal*. He accepts that I edit an email 15 times before pressing send. I accept that he crunches pita chips at ear-splitting decibels. He accepts that I recover from night terrors with epic intervals of trash TV.

Just be sure to be clear about your boundaries. And have fun!

Dear Laura,

I dreamt a tree was growing in my vagina, branches creaking into my fallopian tubes. I think it means the cancer's back. I'm not ready to lose my lady parts. I can't bring myself to make the appointment.

~*Fearing the Cleaver*

Dear Cleaver,

I understand your reluctance to submit yourself to the chopping block. Medical professionals dole out a pound of pain with an ounce of cure. They treat your cancer, but take your lady parts. They stabilize your moods, but lock you in slug mode. Sometimes it seems better to cope with body drama on your own.

That said: doctors use excellent testing apparatuses. You should at least take advantage of their medical machinations to divine the accuracy of your dream. After all, unconscious worlds deceive: I keep dreaming I hear a baby crying in the closet, suffocating under sweaters and shoes. I tear through sneakers, jackets, slips, scarves, and blue jeans. But by the time I find her, it's too late: she's suffocated.

I wake up foggy of head, and a creeping sense of unease seeps into the day. But I speculate the dream reveals no more than the peril of pickle-and-almond butter sandwiches as a midnight snack. And while I trust you tread wiser gastronomical waters, perhaps your dream heralds not cancer but positive growth. Trees can suggest creativity, fertility, or new life. That's what I hope your future holds. In the meantime, however: make that appointment!

Dear Laura,

I respect Tim's appreciation for fresh squirrel meat, and he tolerates my preference for cucumber sandwiches. Pocahontas is the problem. He met this chick with dark braids at a brain-tanning class and he goes foraging with her on a weekly basis. I'm worried that they might be foraging for more than roots and berries, if you get my drift.

~*Indoorsy*

Dear Indoorsy,

Maybe you should ask to join them on one of their "expeditions." From observing their interactions, you can get a sense of whether their relationship is carnal or platonic. Also, it could give you a chance to experience the great outdoors through your husband's eyes.

Dear Laura,

I was moping around the living room, doing half-hearted wheelies in my electric wheelchair, when my dad tossed *The Brothers Karamazov* in my lap. It was hard to get into, and I mostly just flipped through, laughing at his dorky marginalia. Then I read this passage:

> *Love every leaf, every ray of light. Love the animals, love the plants, love everything. If you love everything, you will perceive the divine mystery in things. Once you perceive it, you will begin to comprehend it better every day. And you will come at last to love the world with an all-embracing love.*

Then the dead skin shattered off the living room furniture and underneath was a love so unbearable I wept. I realized, suddenly, my heart bursting, that there was no heart of darkness at my center, and there was no heart of darkness at the center of anyone else. The wallpaper shone like the sun.

Then, this morning, it was gone. While waiting in the rain for the bus to lower the wheelchair ramp, life felt meaningless again. What happened?

~Lucy in San Francisco

Dear Lucy,

A psychiatrist might say you had a brief bipolar flare, but I think you had an experience of grace. The love you felt *is* the only true thing, and it *has* been there the whole time. It is the ground of being on which we stand.

For some reason, though, being human involves only seeing it in creaks and glances. We lend our cell phone to a migrant worker who just stepped off the bus from Oaxaca, and experience a "thin" moment where this love seeps through. The next day our in-laws surprise us with a dog-meat ugly couch, and we stew for fourteen hours, cooking thoroughly in a Crock-Pot of wrath.

I think Dostoevsky already gave you your answer—you know, the whole loving every grain of sand thing. Which is borderline impossible when you're waiting for a wheelchair ramp to descend in the rain. But—according to most randomized double-blind scientific studies—that's when it counts the most.

Dear Laura,

On the turnpike, he asked the tollbooth attendant for a three-way. At the wharf, he wanted to do it in a bucket of shark chum. I just woke up in a vat of creamed corn with a circus peanut in every orifice. Help! This is getting out of hand.

> ~Beached (and desperate)
> Whale in Trenton

Dear Trenton,

Your husband may be suffering from a sexual addiction, or—since these are new predilections—a degenerative neurological disorder. Either way—for your sake, at least—he needs some psychiatric/medical evaluation, ASAP. No one deserves to wake up with a circus peanut in every orifice. No one.

Dear Laura,

Tim was startled when I invited myself along for the truffle-hunting expedition, and Pocahontas looked distinctly uncomfortable. Five miles from the trailhead, I tripped over a tree root and dislocated my knee. While my husband orienteered his way to the ranger station, Pocahontas made a splint from a tree branch and her bandana. While I whimpered, she told me she admired me for braving the wilderness, since her own girlfriend (whose picture she showed me in her cell phone) wouldn't even step out the door without high heels.

Guess I was worried over nothing.

> ~Indoorsy

Dear Indoorsy,

Glad things worked out. I hope your husband brings you tea sandwiches on a silver tray while you are in recovery! I have been taking advantage of this pregnancy to demand room service at will. Milk that knee for all it's worth!

Dear Laura,

The doctor took note that Darrel has been using Skeet-B-Gone, a small, clip-on device that disperses a "cocoon" of bug protection around the wearer. As this mist also contains a mild neurotoxin with psychotropic effects, it was likely the source of Darrel's transgressive sexual urges. The good doctor traded Darrell's Skeet-B-Gone for a year's supply of tranquilizers. My husband—and our sex life—should be back to vanilla in no time.

~*Freed Whale in Trenton*

Dear Trenton,

Your story makes a compelling public service message about the dangers of Skeet-B-Gone. Sucks to have lived it, though. I wonder what your husband will think of the ordeal when restored to his right mind. Do you plan to start the roleplay conversation all over again? Or are you frightened away from fantasyland for good?

Dear Laura,

I've come to the conclusion that the universe is cold and cruel and devoid of meaning, that consciousness is an infinitesimal accident of space-time, and that Dostoevsky is full of shit. Just as surely as Fyodor's literary genius was an accident of epilepsy, my "moment of grace" was a waterfall of dopamine reactors. I'm going to go eat a tub of mayonnaise in front of the TV now, and hope that cholesterol kills me before paralysis sets in.

~*Lucy in San Francisco*

Believe me, Lucy:

I understand your temptation to nihilism. Earth's cries of silent injustice suggest an apathetic God. We imitate God in ignoring these screams. They seep into our pocketbooks (burgeoned by the infrastructure of oppression), our cheeseburgers (once cows wallowing in cesspools), and our jeans (stitched in tight quarters by cramped hands).

The premise of this forum is that the psychiatric limitations we experience should open our capacity for joy; that we must boldly fight the currents of self-recrimination our depressive flesh is heir to.

But if we're drinking Malbec while children are dying of dysentery, maybe we SHOULD feel like shit.

If we're helping the rich get into Harvard, thus ensuring their continued hegemony, maybe we SHOULD feel like gnarled stumps oozing with mycelium.

I'll just come out and say it: EVERYONE should be depressed by the waitress's sad eyes and unethically sourced shrimp. Lucy in San Francisco: you are absolutely right. What good does it do to know that an undercurrent of love runs through everything if you can't FEEL it? What good does it do to acknowledge that this love is real if you don't also acknowledge that LOVE DEMANDS JUSTICE?

You know who wasn't very upbeat?

ANY prophet.

EVER.

Maybe my husband shouldn't accept that, post-nightmare, I binge-watch *Bridalplasty*. Maybe he should ask me about my dreams—visions of suffering. Maybe my dreams are prophecies: prophecies that the bread in my cupboard belongs to the hungry man; the coat in my closet belongs to the man with no coat; the shoes rotting on my shelf belong to the man with no shoes; the money in my bank belongs to the poor.

That's Basil of Caesarea, folks. Circa 300 AD. We've known this shit for a long, long, time.

I'm tearing coats out of my closet.

I'm handing out twenties in the Walmart parking lot.

I just went online and adopted fifteen African orphans.

When my husband comes home, I'm going to tell him, with shaking hands and beating heart:

There must be another way to live.

Dear Laura,

I used to have pert, athletic, breasts and a slender frame. Then I got depressed and gained 15 pounds of voluptuous hips. Swallowing pink birth control tablets made my breasts mutate to Ds.

I lack a sultry voice, a voluptuous personality. I carry my large breasts awkwardly, as if someone has strapped two flagons of mead to my ribcage. Help!

~*D-cup in Detroit*

Dear D-cup,

Can I say something?

First world problem!

And I'm, um, sorry it took me so long to answer your post. Word to the wise, folks: it's not a good idea for EVERYONE to go off their meds when pregnant. Sometimes the real risk to the baby is that, five months in, Mommy will fire her therapist, quit her job, and threaten her husband with divorce if he doesn't pack his bags for an agrarian commune in Pensacola, FL, to squeeze out an equitable existence from the rocky soil. Ha ha!

To answer your question: I have no fucking clue. Turns out, *D-cup*: I don't have the answers. While I know we need radical solutions to respond to the crisis of the present moment—whether it be excessive cleavage or the socio-political infrastructure of oppression—it turns out my solutions tend to be crazy.

That said, a good sports bra would probably help.

Dear Laura,

My dream was right: the cancer's back. Docs say I've got three months. Problem is, I don't know anything more about life than I did at seventeen. My mind is still crumpled with orange rinds and wadded papers. I've borne three children, danced the tango on the shores of Costa Rica, and restored seventeen miles of Snowy Plover habitat. Still: I feel like I've wasted my life.

~*Fearing the Reaper*

Dear Reaper,

They say you die like you live.

This, if you ask me, is a crushing disappointment. Facing the gaping jaws of eternity, shouldn't we stop sweating the small stuff and join the general dance? It makes for an anti-climactic end if the jetsam that generally rattles through our head still circles as our heartbeats slow and still.

As I said to D-cup: I don't have the answers. I do have a daughter kicking at my bladder; a beautiful, pure (and soon to be shit-squirting) being who will, in another month or so, pickaxe her way through my perineum. I feel like when I hear her laugh, everything will be okay.

Sartre said hell is other people.

Sartre was an asshole.

We all know loving one another is the whole goddamn point of this human condition. So spend these last moments with your children. Let them stroke your cheek, wash your hair, kiss you goodbye. After all, maybe you're the lucky one. Being human is rough stuff. You get to be done.

Signing off, for now and always,

~Laura Freedman

✳ IN THE HALL OF OLD ✳ TESTAMENT MIRACLES

A Horror Story by Cody Splunk

Everyone knows that the first second you're alone with a wax sculpture, it's going to try to kill you. So why bring the Bible to life with 300 wax figures that are just *waiting* to hunt us down with shepherd's crooks and slay us in a manger?

"Because you live in Kentucky," Janice said.

"Okay. Right. Are you sure this is a good idea?"

"Would you rather swing back to Fluff & Ed's for another gravel burger? Eat ice cream bars in the Dairy Queen parking lot?" Janice swiped a credit card through the lock. "And we're in!"

"Ice cream bars sound nice."

She pulled me into the pitch-black museum.

"Shouldn't you, like, be avoiding trespassing? What with your background situation, et cetera?"

"Good God, Cody!" She clicked her flashlight on. "I've been living a buckled down, bed-making life for a year! The most fun in my life is watching television! Television! You've been subsidizing the very expensive whims of the *entire* Splunk clan. We deserve a little danger slash fun. A little dangerfun."

"I've never been a huge fan of dangerfun."

"That's why you're a virgin."

"You get mean after a beer."

"You know who else was a virgin?"

I didn't say anything.

"Mary, Queen of Heaven! Plus also? Jesus!" She ruffled my hair. "Besides, only virgins can ride unicorns." She scanned the area with her flashlight. "Costumes!" She walked unevenly towards them and pawed through the rack. "I am, of course, your tour guide." She slipped into a robe, pulled on a headdress, and struck a pose. "Do I look like Mary Magdalene?"

The headscarf covered the piercings, the cherry red highlights. She looked like Joan of Arc, but with mascara.

"The resemblance is uncanny."

"Alright then. Into the beckoning dark."

Janice pulled a wall lever, dimly illuminating each diorama in the Life of Christ exhibit. "And they bought him at Toys "R" Us, wrapped him in a swaddling cloth, and laid him in a manger." Baby doll Jesus was ringed by a papier mâché camel, a taxidermy donkey, and a cow reclining on hay-scattered cement. A manikin angel torso was glued midway up the wall, indicating flight.

"Did you know that St. Francis made the first nativity scene?" Janice asked.

"No."

"He wanted to make Jesus accessible."

"Did he use manikins?"

"No. Which was, perhaps, the key to his success." Janice observed the pale, unnatural figures. "Kind of makes 1st century Palestine seem like J.C. Penny."

We paused before a diorama depicting Jesus's temptation in the desert. A cloaked and hooded devil stood opposite Jesus in a field of papier mâché rocks.

Janice punched a button and made a theatrical gesture. "Voila!" The background of the diorama lit up red, and the speakers crackled, releasing a community theater rendition of King James text. Jesus had a southern drawl, and the Devil's voice was digitally distorted, like when they disguise a mob informant on TV.

Narrator: Then the devil taketh him up into an exceedingly high mountain, and sheweth him all the kingdoms of the world, and the glory of them; and saith unto him:

Devil: *(Watery distortion.)* All these things will I give thee, if thou wilt fall down and worship me.

Narrator: Then saith Jesus unto him:

Jesus: Get thee hence, Satan. *(Thunder. Lightning.)* For it is written, Thou shalt worship the Lord thy God, and him only shalt thou serve.

Narrator: Then the devil leaveth him, and, behold, angels came and ministered unto him.

The speaker crackled off.

"Sounds like Satan's in the witness protection program," I said.

"Wise choice, here in the rhinestone buckle of the Bible Belt."

"It's weird that the devil is quoting scripture. It's like he's working within Jesus's framework. Which you wouldn't expect."

"The devil is a logician," Janice said.

"Meaning?"

"Logic can't save you."

"Don't knock it 'til you've tried it."

"Ha."

We approached a stone well, where a wax Jesus sat conversing with a scraggly-haired, ruby-lipped manikin.

"The woman at the well," Janice said. "See, Jesus is transcending a social boundary by reaching out to a woman. And a non-Jewish woman at that."

"You know your Bible."

"Youth group served good snacks."

We observed wax Jesus in silence. He had silky blonde hair and Aryan features.

"Yeah," Janice said. "Bible Walk didn't get the memo that Jesus was black."

"Why's the girl all mangy?"

"I think her permed and color-treated hair is supposed to represent a life of sin."

"Hopefully Jesus recommends a good conditioner."

As we stood there, the female manikin's mangy wig slipped off. It landed at her feet, and lay there like a sick cat.

"God, that's creepy," Janice said. "Should we put it back on?"

"No!"

"Don't be a sissy, Splunk." Janice picked up the wig. She secured it on the manikin's head. "There you go, dear."

"When they find our bones in the manger tomorrow morning, you get the blame." I surveyed the dimly lit hall. "So what's next? Let's fastforward."

"Miracles. Healings. Crucifixion. Resurrection." We strolled past wax Jesus healing lepers, raising the dead, dying on a cross.

"What about, like, the Sermon on the Mount stuff?"

"They kind of skip the social gospel. No 'for I was thirsty and you gave me to drink, I was in prison and you visited me.' It's more about getting saved."

We stood before the final diorama, where Jesus sat on a throne between heaven and hell, wearing a crown, inspecting the lamb's book of life. A secretary manikin in a sweater vest roasted in a fiery hole with rubber rats and plastic iguanas. On the right, heaven's residents enjoyed fields of plastic tulips. A mural depicted heaven's living arrangements: a colonial mansion and modern luxury condominiums.

"If it's all about getting saved, it seems selfish," I said.

"Yeah, they should end with a wax Afghani child with her leg blown off and an immigrant dying in the desert and have them all saying 'Hey, guess what? Ha ha, sort of awkward, but actually? I'm Jesus.'"

"Do they have a suggestion box?"

Janice took my hand and swung it playfully as we backtracked through the Life of Christ exhibit. "So what's next? Want to see the unicorns from Noah's Ark?"

"You're kidding."

"Two of them. Plus Pterodactyls! And we haven't even gone through the Gauntlet of Christian Martyrs. Which is disappointingly un-gruesome, incidentally. I've seen gorier statuettes in—"

I stopped short, staring at the woman at the well. Who was now standing up.

Janice halted. "What?"

"Baldy moved."

Janice regarded the scene. "I'm pretty sure it was like that before."

"We need to leave, stat."

"But you haven't even seen the Founding Fathers."

"I thought this was a Bible museum."

"Fundamentalists are into Founding Fathers," Janice said. "Don't you watch—"

She froze.

I followed her gaze to the manger. Which was empty.

"Are you fucking with me, Splunk?"

"I didn't—"

A clattering sound came from the hall.

"Night Janitor," Janice whispered. "Split up and hide."

"Bad idea." But she'd already slipped into the darkness.

I bolted around the corner and flattened myself against the wall, scanning the area for movement. The display to my left featured Jesus surrounded by multiracial children and taxidermy mammals. To my right, a table of twelve wax disciples broke bread in suspended animation.

Step, drag.

Footsteps emanated from around the corner.

Step, drag.

A figure staggered into sight: a female form in Bible-era robes.

I stepped forward. "Janice?"

The figure turned, knocking off its wig.

Baldy.

AUUUGHHHHHHHHHHHHHH!!!!!!!

My blood-curdling wail was like an evil alarm clock, inciting rustling throughout the room. An Asian child clambered unevenly off Jesus' lap. Wax Judas cocked his head to the side and rose unnaturally from the disciple's table. Baby doll Jesus skittered towards me in a fiendish crawl.

Weapon. I needed a weapon. Last supper baguette: no. Wooden chalice: no. I grabbed a faux-silver candlestick and rushed the field, evading Baldy's awkward tackle. As I sprinted past the manger scene, the Virgin Mary stood up, the blank marbles of her eyes following me as I dashed into the hall. I crouched behind a gift shop display case, catching my breath among slogan-emblazoned mugs:

Try Jesus. If you don't like him, the devil will always take you back.

FBI: Firm Believer in Christ.

Greater love has no man than this: that he lay down his life for a friend.

My spine tingled with a dawning awareness: I was not alone. I clasped my useless candlestick.

A hand grasped me from behind. "Don't scream."

"Janice. Thank God."

"Who were you expecting? Baldy?"

"Actually, yes."

Janice had traded her Bible robes for a shirt that read: *God Doesn't Believe in Atheists.*

"That doesn't make sense."

"My *shirt* doesn't make sense?" She yanked me past display cases to the cash register counter. We ducked behind it, as Jesus and the disciples shambled into the gift shop, forming an ungainly herd.

"So where are the exits?" I asked.

We watched a wax Judas drag his unearthly feet over to Jesus and Bartholomew. They stood in a triumvirate by the costume display, as if conversing.

"Um," Janice said. "They're kind of leaning on it."

"Janice! You should have left when you had the chance."

"I had to find you first, screamy McGee. Anyway, we can still make a run for it. I mean, what can they actually do to us?"

A flaxen-haired angel manikin shambled up to the waxen triumvirate. Its head bobbed, its body moving in eager undulation.

Wax Judas raised his arms like a drawbridge, placed them against the angel manikin's neck. And broke his head off. The angel head bounced across the floor. The waxen herd turned their heads, following its trajectory.

"Okay, so they can snap our heads off," Janice said.

"I'm a little concerned that Jesus didn't intervene," I said.

"That's not Jesus," Janice said.

"Looks like Jesus."

"Jesus was nonviolent."

"And, presumably, not made of evil wax."

"Old Testament Miracles might have an emergency exit."

"Weapons. We need weapons."

"Braille Bible?" Janice proffered a clothbound book.

"I was thinking broadsword. Or battleaxe."

"AUUUUUGHHHHHHHH!" Janice slammed the Bible against her foot, where Baby Doll Jesus was gnawing through her jeans.

I dove for a grip on his belly, but his thrashing feet scratched my wrists and bruised my arms. Blood ran from his tiny baby lips as I wrenched him from her ankle and hucked him over the counter.

The waxen herd turned their collective heads toward us.

Janice looked very pale. "He bit me, Cody."

Come on, babe," I said. "It's miracle time."

In the Hall of Old Testament Miracles, Joseph and his manikin brothers gnawed on Thomas Jefferson, who flailed his wax arms helplessly.

"He must have wandered over from the other wing," Janice whispered.

I nodded at Cain, who was staggering towards us with a bloody rock. "Sprint!"

We dashed past the Garden of Eden and the prow of an Ark. "Quick! In here," Janice said, pulling me into the dark crevice of a whale's mouth. We watched Cain stagger by, marble eyes shifting. Israelites milled about a Styrofoam Mount Sinai, while Moses wandered around a pillar of salt with his tablets, looking lost.

"Check out Abraham and Isaac." Janice nodded at a bearded patriarch, who was chopping at a wax boy tangled in rope.

"Is he murdering him or freeing him?"

"Unclear." Janice nodded at the mountain. "We've got to go up and over."

A taxidermy lion stalked by, manikin martyr head in his mouth.

Janice yanked up a wooden board painted with waves. "Here's your broadsword," she said. She pulled up another. "And here's my battleaxe."

We ran at Mount Sinai, suffering a barrage of manikin karate chops. Swinging our boards wildly, we stumbled up the precipice. Our feet punched through Styrofoam, failed to find footing. By the time we crested the summit, we were surrounded on all sides.

"Shit!" Janice said, thwacking Moses over the beard. "This was not the plan."

"Go back to Egypt!" I shouted, slamming him on the knees.

I felt a sharp pain against my hip. Bloody-bearded Abraham had buried his axe in my side.

"Save it for your son!" Janice roared, smacking him with her board. The robed patriarch toppled down the mountain, creating a domino effect of falling manikins.

The fiends crept slowly backwards, a tide receding.

"That's right," Janice shouted. "You'd better run."

I looked down at my shorts. They were soaked in blood. I felt a little bit dizzy. Lying down seemed like a good idea. As my skull hit Styrofoam, I saw why the horde had retreated. An armored giant towered above us. His legs were like tree trunks. His curly hair brushed the ceiling. He clutched a bronze spear.

"Janice," I said. I pointed.

"Of course." Janice threw up her arms. "They have a Goliath."

My side hurt. A lot.

Janice looked around. "Cody, you wouldn't happen to have five smooth round stones?"

"Styrofoam chunk?" I feebly tossed a papier mâché rock at the giant. It glanced off his head.

The giant raised his right hand and karate-chopped the mountain. Janice and I tumbled down the crumbling Styrofoam. I hit my head on the cement. Goliath raised his left leg, and brought it down in a mighty stomp. Janice rolled out of the way just in time.

"Rope!" I cried. "Rope!"

Janice yanked up an extension cord that was masking-taped to the ground.

"Tie his legs!" I yelled. I grabbed a shepherd's crook. "Hey, Goliath! I waved the shepherd's crook maniacally. "That's right, you Philistine!" The giant cocked his head to the side. "You have no appreciation for art or music!"

Janice struggled to knot the cord around his tree-trunk ankle.

"Think Ewoks versus Walkers in *Return of the Jedi*!"

"That means nothing to me!"

Goliath raised his spear.

"Run around his legs with the rope!"

Goliath brought his spear smashing down on my foot. Splintering pain. I crumpled into a pile of rubble. Dazed, I watched Janice run around and around him with the rope.

"Yank it!" I yelled.

She yanked.

Goliath wobbled. Stumbled. And came crashing down. The cement floor shook. A plume of grey mountain dust rose in his wake.

"Fiends!" Janice jumped atop Goliath's fallen frame. "We have bested your champion. Now let us go in peace!"

The creatures stood there, undulating.

My toe hurt a lot.

"Good. I'm glad to know that, despite being evil minions of hell, you have some sense of honor."

Slowly, painfully, I stood up.

"Good luck with the whole being evil thing." Janice nodded to the horde. "Hope it works out for you."

They rushed us.

"Supply closet!" Janice yelled. She dove behind Noah's ark, yanked open a painted-black door. "Quick, get in!"

I dove.

Janice yanked the door shut.

"Phew," she said, turning the lock, flipping on a light switch.

We both leaned against the door.

"Maybe we can last the night in here," I said. "Those things have got to freeze up in sunlight."

Janice glanced at her watch. "Three A.M."

"Great. Two hours."

A scratching sound came from the other side of the door.

"Not good," Janice said.

The scratching became thudding.

"Shit," Janice said.

THUD.

"I love you," I said.

"Splunk, this is not—." Her face grew pale. "Shit! You're bleeding all over the place!"

I slumped over. "The . . . moon."

Janice followed my gaze to a small, dusty, window.

THUD.

Janice stacked cardboard boxes. She climbed the wobbling tower.

THUD.

Janice pulled off her shirt and wound it around her hand. She pulled back her shirt-gloved fist, and shattered the window.

THUD.

Shards of glass stuck from the edges.

There was a scratching, splintering noise. An axe came through the door.

"Cody!"

"Go," I moaned.

"I'll get help," she shouted, and wriggled out the window.

I watched the axe splinter through the door.

Saving the girl you love from evil manikins, I thought. *Not the worst way to go.*

The hole grew. Outside it, manikins and wax figures undulated homicidally.

Even the mug said it. Greater love hath no man than this.

Judas stuck his arm through the hole, blind hand swatting at the lock.

But you know what would also be nice?

Hot wax fingers gripped the knob.

Living.

Musket fire.

Being loved back.

A blur of white. Manikins slammed to the ground. Horse hooves as big as my face crashed through the door. A blazing white unicorn reared before me.

Through her legs, I saw a militia of minutemen driving back the Old Testament figures. George Washington was stabbing wax Moses with a bayonet, and Moses was defending himself with awkward tablet swings. Baby Doll Jesus gnawed at Patrick Henry's wig, while Patrick Henry swatted at him with the Declaration of Independence. Ben Franklin strangled Baldy with the string of his kite. Flailing, she karate-chopped his bloomers.

On the splintered door, wax Judas stirred. Floundered upright. Loomed over me, axe raised.

Eyes flashing, the unicorn drove her horn through Judas's chest. She flung him against the Ark. Judas crumpled lifelessly to the cement, a gaping hole where his heart should have been.

Cain clutched his bloody rock, eyes shifting.

The unicorn bared her teeth at the original brother-killer and roared.

Cain dropped his rock. Hobbled away.

The unicorn stood over me, eyes wild.

"Please don't kill me."

She sniffed my neck. Nickered. Her warm breath was like the spring.

I touched her blazing hide. It was soft as cornsilk, fiery and alive.

Boosting myself with a box, I clambered onto the unicorn's back. An ocean breeze rippled through her mane and her horn radiated dazzling light.

We galloped through the horde of karate-chopping manikins, into the blazing sunshine.

✷ FAUX ROSE ✷

Day 1

Pain has shattered this moment, made it the thinnest between life and death, this world and the next. Pushing her into the cold dry bright world: this is the most alive you will ever be. This is the sharp clear peak of your life. Rose, you were a clump of cells splitting and dividing, renewing yourself in time. You have knit yourself into a person—sputtering, smeared in white. You squish your eyes closed, nuzzling and rooting for the nipple, perturbation on your tiny perfect face. Black eyes, infinitesimal fingernails. Cause to rejoice: Our junk works. Our love has sprouted and grown leaves. We have made a perfect thing.

Day 2

Feels like someone took a cheese grater to my perineum. Elaborate bathroom spray-bottle hygiene required to keep wound from infecting. I can barely walk. Rose suckles weakly. Nurse keeps asking how many ounces she drank. *How the hell should I know, bitch?* "Two ounces," I say, pulling numbers from the black hole of constipation I once knew as my ass.

"Maybe we should try some formula," the nurse says.

"No fucking way," I say.

The nurse looks concerned. "Have you slept?"

"Breast is best," I say.

"Why don't I take her to the nursery? You can get some shut-eye. Your body needs rest."

"NO."

The nurse stares at me.

"I'll sleep better with her here."

Pink horse pills after dinner.

Day 3

An itching in my nerves. A frantic energy filling my joints, every cell allergic to itself. This buzzing light, fluorescence, crazy amoebas multiplying on walls.

I need to get up. Out. Take Rose and run. I swing my legs over the side of the bed. It feels like someone shoved a pole up my vagina. Rivers of blood leaking out. Some splatters to the floor.

"You're bleeding honey," Ben says.

"We need to go. Where's Rose?"

"Lie down, babe."

"Get Rose. We need to leave."

"Okay," Ben says, loping out of the room. He returns with the nurse.

"What's the matter, honey?"

"I want to see my baby."

The nurse touches Ben on the arm. "I'm going to get her something to calm down."

"I can hear you, fatty."

They ram me full of something else. I fall asleep.

Day 4

"That's not my baby," I say.

The nurse examines the baby's wristband. "It's your baby, ma'am."

"I think I would know."

"Read the wristband, Ms. Freedman."

"I see the wristband. My point is, the wristband is wrong."

The nurse scoops the baby from my lap. Walks briskly from the room.

"I can't believe she fucked up the wrist bands," I say. "Usually hospitals are so careful about those things."

Ben looks lost. "Honey, that was Rose."

"She smells different."

"You haven't slept."

"HER EYES ARE A DIFFERENT COLOR."

Ben sits on the bed. Wraps his arms around me. "Honey," he says.

"Goddamn it, Ben." I struggle free, grasp the bed railing, stand up. "Do I have to do everything myself?"

The nurse is back. "You need to stay in bed, ma'am." She is armed with a needle, a young female doctor.

"You need to bring us our ACTUAL CHILD." I turn to the doctor. "Miss. Your colleague made a wristband error. She mixed up our babies, which, I'm sure, was an accident. A clerical error. But we need to get this straightened out before some other couple takes *our* baby home."

The nurse tries to get me back into bed, but I fight her. The doctor holds my arm down. A pinprick, sedation. I see groggy lumps of fuzz-people. I pass through a veil of light, and am knee-deep in a pink and humming lake, nursing my real baby. Rose. Black-eyed Rose. I love her so much it burns my heart.

Day 5

I wake up with the cold knowledge I can't act crazy: I must feed it, the false, squirming thing. I must boldly mime to the doctor they called in: I subscribe to the consensus (conspiracy). Two plus two is five. I love Big Brother. Really. I am giving her my teat. She sucks away successfully. More evidence she's not Real Rose.

"I'd like to walk down to the cafeteria," I say to Ben.

"I'll go with you."

"Stay here. Watch the baby. I need to stretch my legs."

I creep down the hall, scouring rooms not my own. All wrong, these babies. Not mine, not mine, not mine. An ache grows in my stomach; a cannon blast of dread. I am too late.

I take the elevator to the parking lot. Maybe they are just now loading her in. Maybe I can catch them, snatch her back. I creep barefoot through the cars. No Rose. No Rose. No Rose.

I lie down on the pavement. Dear God, I say. Please.

If I lie here, keeping vigil, maybe they will bring her back.

They gather me from the ground. Ben makes calls to my brother, my counselor, my psychiatrist. Dear God. The whole parade. The psychiatrist says: fuck breastfeeding, get her back on Seroquel, *now*.

Day 6

The anxiety eating at me won't let me sit or eat. Rest means missed opportunity to find her: real Rose. So I pace, milk bleeding through my shirt.

The psych ward nurse has bifocal glasses and a freckled chest. She asks me if I won't sit with her, talk a bit.

We sit. I delineate the situation with clear eyes and shaking hands. I entreat her to bring me list of maternity ward births in the last week.

She listens with kind eyes.

"I need to find my daughter," I say. "I don't think I can live without her."

"You need to stay still," she says. "So you can heal."

It still feels like shearing scissors have sliced through my perineum. Real Rose tore me up down there.

"If you heal," she says. "You can do a better job finding your daughter." She pats my arm. "Think about that."

Patronizing, she has a point. Must muffle crazy. I put on real clothes, lipstick. Wash and comb my hair. Sit on a couch in the lounge, pretend to read. This lasts fifteen minutes.

There's a fire inside me. I go back to agitated pacing. I've got to get out.

Day 7

"You haven't asked to see Rose," Ben says, sitting on my bed, holding my hand.

"I have not stopped asking to see Rose," I say. "You have betrayed me in the deepest possible way."

"I meant the real Rose."

"So did I."

As soon as I get Real Rose back: divorce, divorce, divorce.

"I suppose you're bottle feeding that other thing."

"You mean our daughter? Well, hon, I *am* bottle feeding our daughter. You know why? I don't have any fucking breasts."

The kind-eyed nurse looks up from her station.

"Technically you do have breasts. I mean, you have nipples."

"I'm sorry." He puts his head down on the bed. "This is a nightmare."

"Tell me about it."

Day 8

Keep me the fuck away from Faux Rose. They met without me, my betraying benefactors, and decided. Keep me locked up and away from the bathtub, the paring knife, the pawnshop gun. Pump me full of Seroquel—ram the antipsychotic up my veins until I'm a cheese log, a dented spoon, a kite.

Small orange pills, with orange juice, every morning.

Day 9

I stopped talking about it. No one believes me, anyway.

Day 10

They wheel us out of the hospital, spokes of the wheelchair glinting. It is wrong, wrong, wrong.

Day 11

They let me hold Faux Rose. I feel for her what I would feel for a stick of firewood, a mound of clay.

Day 12

The freezer burgeons with casserole. Kin and kindred deliver white lasagna, cornflake chicken, bean and rice. *You must be exhausted,* they say, studying my face. One neighbor rang and ran, leaving a flat of birthday cupcakes on the bristly mat. They were store-bought—chemical frosting, stuck through with plastic clown heads and candy angel wings. Cupcake purgatory.

I mash the cupcakes in the outside trash bin, alongside diapers smeared with mustardy poop. I picture myself laying Faux Rose on the cupcake mountain, shutting the bin, walking away.

Maybe it would bring Real Rose back.

✹ HURRY UP PLEASE, IT'S TIME ✹

"I just need to sleep," your wife told you three days ago. "I need you to hold me while I sleep." She came out of the bathroom naked, her stomach pouchy, breasts swollen and leaking milk. You took off your clothes. You held each other under the covers. Your wife was shaking and crying. She asked for the baby. She held Rose close to her, nuzzled against her neck. You kissed them both. You left for work.

When you came back, they were gone.

Stupid. So stupid. She had stopped the *it's not my baby* talk, but you saw the dark wheels cranking in her mind. She cared for the baby mechanically, changing and feeding a doll. She stared at the wall, watching some slow horror unfold.

"Are you okay, honey?"

"No."

"What's the matter?"

"I can't explain."

You close your eyes: she is drowning Rose in a motel bathtub, driving her slowly into a lake. *Don't let her hurt the baby. Don't let her hurt the baby.*

Two days later, a policeman calls.

You suck in your breath. Sit down on a chair.

He says: I think we found your baby, sir.

Rose was abandoned in a gas station bathroom. Dehydrated, otherwise okay.

And now a girl in a skeleton hoodie is at the door, handing you your wife's journal. "Janice," she says, sticking out her hand. "I got two days off work, I can help with the flyers."

"Can you hold her?" you ask the girl, trading baby for journal. Your wife's neat, even, handwriting is on the cover. *Laura's Journal of Mystery and Wonder. McAllen, Texas. August 2004.* "I'm not supposed to read this," you say.

The girl jiggles Rose, humming deep and low. Rose sputters, hiccups. Blinks open her eyes.

You set the journal on the coffee table, go into the kitchen for a drink. Your wife's best friend hands you a glass of amber liquid. You down it. She gives you a hug. "Ben," she says. "This is not your fault." Then she goes back to stacking flyers emblazoned with photos of your wife. *Missing. Reward.* In the pictures she is laughing, wearing lipstick. She looks normal. She looks fine.

At night you push the baby around the neighborhood, the neighborhood your wife thought was perfect. "Downward mobility!" she shouted, laughing too loud. Most people in this neighborhood have only odd jobs, and she liked this. She called it downward mobility, but it was more like playing poor, with family purse strings within easy tugging distance. You pass a yard with five chihuahuas wearing striped, collared shirts. They throw themselves against the chain link fence, barking wildly.

Someone is sleeping in a scratched white Chevy. It is the skeleton girl. Sleeping in her shitty car. You knock on the window. She sits straight up, startled. It takes her a moment to recognize you. She rolls down the window. "Yeah?"

You don't know why you knocked. "Aren't you cold?"

"I'm okay."

"We have an extra bedroom."

She evaluates your face. Shrugs.

Inside, you show her the spare room, into which your wife banished your GameCube, your TV. Corded monsters, she called them. Vampires of the inner life.

"I can take the baby," the girl says. "If you want to get some rest." She flops on the bed, pats her stomach.

You lay the baby on her. Sit down on a rocking chair. "How do you know Laura?"

"I was a feral raccoon who drove her to madness." She watches your reaction. "She was my English teacher."

You rub your eyes.

"I was at the wedding, actually."

The wedding.

Your cheeks grow wet.

"Have you been bargaining?"

"I'm sorry?"

"I've been bargaining. If they find her safe, I have to go to say a rosary every day for the rest of my life."

"I don't believe in God."

"I don't believe in bargaining." She kisses Rose's head. "I always bargain, though."

"I thought she could do it. I thought if she tried harder. If I tried harder."

"Some things you can't do by trying."

"What else is there?"

Janice slowly strokes Rose's head. "You should sleep."

"I can't sleep."

"Then read the journal." Janice uses her right foot to push off her left tennis shoe. "Maybe there's a clue."

I sit there.

"Want to get the light?" Janice says.

"Okay." You stand up. Flip the switch.

"You'll find her, Ben," Janice says into the dark.

In the living room, you pour yourself another. Lay down on sofa. Open your wife's journal. Read.

✵ RESURRECTION SNOW GLOBE ✵

Laura's Journal of Mystery & Wonder
McAllen, Texas ~ August 2004

August 16

Billboards of note on the drive down to McAllen:

"Vaginal Rejuvenation—Experience Love again!"

"Club Fantasy Gentleman's Club, TOTALLY EXPOSED! Girls! Sports! Fried Fish Buffet!"

"Need Directions?—GOD"

My roommates: three volunteers in their second year, already on the verge of escaping to grad school/med school/law school. The house—a dilapidated former convent—has stored volunteers since the program's Texas inception. I dump my stuff in the small yellow room upstairs, jimmy open windows with a butcher knife, smash cockroaches with empty jars. The room bears marks of residents past: a window box of geranium skeletons. Empty prescription bottles in the trash. Downstairs, there is an empty, humid chapel and a weight room with antiquated hand weights, a full-length mirror, and a poster of a muscled Jesus doing a push up with the cross on his back. *Sins of the world,* the poster reads. *Try bench-pressing this.*

Housemates: Araceli, Margo, and Philip. Araceli irons her shirts, gels her hair into a sleek black ponytail, and deals with the stress of teaching science by running ultramarathons.

Margo teaches kindergarten. She has a resigned expression, sadness bitten in at the lip as she hums tunelessly in the kitchen, chopping chard.

Philip teaches middle school music. He wears a short-sleeved button-down printed with small blue birds. He has grey eyes and a prickly half-beard. On his bookshelf, *Franny and Zooey* leans against *Pedagogy of the Oppressed*.

Am instantly in love.

August 17

Vice principal oriented me to Joseph P. Anderson. Ms. Campos is a sinewy, spiky-haired white lady with an irritated face. She has Texas Longhorns regalia all over her office. She wears beige pantsuits and high heels, and walks around barking into a walkie-talkie.

She scares the shit out of me.

August 18

School mascot: The Anaconda. Large posters line the hallways. "Anacondas are Achievers." A laminated newspaper article is stuck to the wall above the drinking fountain: *Students Need Less Coddling, More Rules and Tasks, Experts Say*. Two girls stare grimly out of the picture, clutching brooms.

There are these metal cage-things that come down and block the halls if there are riots.

Mentor teacher in classroom next door is Mr. Kopecky, a tall, silver-haired man. Came by classroom to give a pep talk. Told story about first job: when nine, he sold pink popcorn at a freak show. One of the freaks was "dogboy," a mute and deformed young man. "I shoved pink popcorn through the bars of his cage," Mr. Kopecky said. "I got fired for feeding pink popcorn to the dog boy."

Not sure how this relates to teaching.

August 19

Eight hours laminating construction paper bear nametags. Because that is what will win them over. Construction paper bears.

August 20

Two hours selecting teacherly outfit. Went with long gray skirt, teal cardigan, and glasses.

I leaned in Philip's doorway. He was sitting in bed, annotating rosters.

"Do I look like a teacher?"

He threw back his head and laughed.

"What?"

"My God. You look like a librarian."

"Why do I feel like I should have a puff paint sweater with addition and subtraction on it? And a denim smock?"

"You're thinking elementary school."

"I feel like an imposter."

"Fake it 'till you make it."

"And here I thought I was supposed to seek authentic selfhood."

"No." Philip said. "Better to be a simulacrum of society's organized despair."

August 22

Mass at Our Lady of Sorrows. While the church is 90% Hispanic, it has a life size Aryan Jesus mannequin hanging from the cross above the altar. The deacon gave a homily about two undocumented immigrants who came to his door, seeking water. He convinced them to turn themselves in to the border patrol.

Dear God!

August 23

"Family dinner" night. Philip made balsamic roasted butternut squash with hot chilies and honey.

On my night, I served Raisin Bran.

August 24

First day of school.

Me: Welcome to English 3. Let's play a game to learn each other's names.

Phil Gasher: We should play boner tag.

Me: That is inappropriate language for the classroom.

Janice Gibbs: Plus boner tag is totally gay.

Me: That is *also* inappropriate language.

Julie Chang: But it's not wrong to be gay, miss. Lots of people are gay.

Danny Ramirez: *(to Julie)* Yeah, like you.

Me: OKAY. We do not use the word *gay* as an insult in this classroom. Using the word gay as an insult perpetuates a negative stereotype. And if you need to say something, you RAISE YOUR HAND.

Kristi Colimote: *(raises hand)*

Me: Kristi?

Kristi Colimote: It's 'cuz on TV, I saw these two chicks getting married and one of them was with short hair and dressed like a dude.

Amelia Basil: *(under breath)* Sodomites!

Me: OKAY. Everyone, grab a pen or pencil from your backpack, and take a look at the worksheet on your desk.

Janice Gibbs: But what about the game, Miss?

Danny Ramirez: Boner tag?

Me: Danny, you just got an hour in ISS.

Danny Ramirez: You laughed when Phil Gasher said it!

Janice Gibbs: Yeah, miss, he can't get in trouble if you laugh.

Me: *(Filling out form.)* Here. You go to ISS. Now.

Danny Ramirez: *(leaving)* You hate me because I'm black!

For the record: Danny is Latino.

August 26

I offered them *A Wrinkle in Time* or *Catcher in the Rye*. I gave a dramatic reading of the first page of each.

"Those books are boring, Miss."

"We should read *Pirates of the Caribbean*."

"I believe that is a movie."

"Nuh-uh Miss. It's even on the shelf."

And indeed. The novelized version of the *Pirates of the Caribbean* film was on the shelf.

"That's not really literature," I said.

August 27

"So I'm reading them a book," I told Philip, "Which was based on a movie. Which was based on a *ride at Disneyland*."

Philip jabbed fork-holes in a yam with assured, graceful stabs. "At least they're listening to you read."

"I mean, if it were the other way around, it would be okay. If there was a Disneyland ride based on *The Catcher in the Rye*, that would be sweet."

Philip picked up my side ponytail and placed it behind my shoulder. I stared at him, touched by the intimate gesture. Disoriented.

"Your hair was in your tea."

I set my mug on the counter. "So it was."

August 31

After school, Ms. Campos came by to yell at me for not being at the curriculum meeting.

"I didn't know there was a curriculum meeting."

"There was a memo in your box."

"I didn't know I had a box."

"C'mon," she said, jerking her head towards the hallway. She led me to a meeting room filled with ELA instructors. "Ms. Freedman wasn't aware there was a curriculum meeting," Ms. Campos said. "Please get her up to speed."

Turns out: I am supposed to be working through a state-issued mass-produced reader, drilling kids on fused sentences and comma splices. While Mr. Kopecky went through slides, I skimmed the reader. After three sentences I wanted to gouge out my eyes.

September 1

"Aw miss, this is boring."

"Why do we have to do this stupid worksheet?"

"We wanna to keep reading our book."

"We wanna write in our journals, miss."

"I don't understand," I said. "When I was reading *Pirates* last week, Danny stuck a fork in the light socket. During journal time last week, Janice tried to light Kristi's hair on fire."

The students looked at me blankly.

"Let's make a deal. As soon as you finish your worksheet, I'll read another chapter."

Worksheets became projectiles. Worksheets became face blotters, spit wads, origami doves, dirty notes on the floor.

"Have it your way," I said. "No *Pirates*. Just more worksheets tomorrow."

"Then we'll just ditch the class, miss."

"Then you'll just get detention, Danny."

"Don't be a hater, miss."

"Don't ditch class, Danny."

"You hate me because I'm black!"

"That doesn't even make any sense," I said. "Class dismissed."

September 2

"What's the point of being a teacher if I'm just supervising rote memorization and worksheet completion?" I said to Philip. "A robot could do that."

He looked up from his grapefruit. "And when they develop the technology to build that robot," he said, "you'll be out of a job."

September 3

Janice Gibbs: a feral child with excessive eye shadow and stringy black hair that obscures her face. I feel a daily urge to take scissors to it. She has an anti-authoritarian complex that would be interesting were it not so ill informed.

During lunch period today, she perched on a desk next to mine.

"What's that you're eating there, miss?"

"Rice and beans."

"Gross."

"I acknowledge it's a little bland. I overcompensate with salt."

"That's gonna make you bloat, Miss."

"It's a risk I'm willing to take. What's for lunch in the cafeteria?"

"Fish sticks. I threw it out."

"What? Fish sticks are fun! You can dip them in ketchup."

"I never eat lunch. I don't eat breakfast either."

"You know that's terrible for you, right?"

"I'm not hungry in the morning. After school I go to Circle K and get Hot Cheetos, a pickle and a Coke."

"Dear God." I handed her my apple. "Please eat this. You're probably about to get scurvy."

"Like the pirates?" she asked, biting into the apple.

"Exactly."

September 6

"Lockdown," Mrs. Gutierrez announced over the intercom this morning. I locked the door, cut the lights, ordered students to get under their desks. Ms.

Campos came by and shook the door handle. It opened. She stepped into the room. "Bang. Bang. Bang," she said, pointing her finger at me. "You're dead."

September 7

Called into Mrs. Gutierrez's office to be redressed for lockdown failure.

Mrs. Gutierrez: All your students are dead.
Me: If it had been a real attack. Yes.
Mrs. Gutierrez: How do you feel about that, Ms. Freedman?
Me: Relieved.
Mrs. Gutierrez: I'm sorry?
Me: Relieved it wasn't a real lockdown!

Mrs. Gutierrez sent me home with a binder on lockdown procedure. Apparently, when a perturbed gunman (or rather, gunchild) bursts into the classroom, the worst thing to do is remain calm. The class should pelt him with a rain of textbooks and pencils. The four burliest students should tackle and disarm him.

Will remember this next time Campos busts in.

September 8

Snooped in Philip's room. A picture of his girlfriend (Tessa) rests on his windowsill in a clear plastic frame. She has russet hair and excellent cheekbones. I turned the picture over.

I don't have to say it, she has written. *You already know.*

What a fucking bitch.

September 9

Lithium side effect: subcutaneous pimples, hard nutty globes of pain. Makes me feel like a decaying leper who should stay in her leper cave, or at least wear a veil in social situations.

Small pink pills, sticking in my throat.

September 10

I strolled through the downtown strip, passing clubwear outlets, taco stands, shops selling bright silk flowers, dollar stores cluttered with quick-dying batteries, blank baseball caps, and nail clippers emblazoned with the Virgin Mary. Girls wearing hoop earrings sat on hot black benches, gentle rolls of belly fat sticking out from midriff tops. Pregnant mothers rolled strollers down Main Street, their kids forking cheese smeared Hot Cheetos from foil bags. Old men in cowboy hats congregated on the corners, thumbs tucked in belt buckles, eyes following legs.

As I walked back to the convent, I saw a woman leaning against the back wall of the rectory, holding the sides of her skirt. Then I noticed the stream of liquid splattering between her legs. "Estoy urinando," she said imploringly. "No hay baños en esas tiendas."

I am peeing. There are no bathrooms in these stores.

September 12

Kristi Colimote, on her boyfriend: My cousin was all, "Do you love him?" And I was like, "Yes." She was like, "If you love him, you'll drink this jar of pickle juice." So I drank it. Then I threw up.

September 13

After dinner, Philip and I sit on the porch, chewing on mesquite pods.
"Do you love your girlfriend?"
"Yes."
"If you love her, you'll drink a jar of pickle juice."
"I don't follow your logic."
"So you're not going to drink it?"
"No. That's disgusting."
"That's what I thought."

September 14

Margo and Araceli invited me to go to South Padre Island Friday night. South Padre is a famous party beach—the kind of place where MTV does its Spring Break show, the kind of place where "Girls Gone Wild" gets filmed. For two weeks in April, it's packed with bikini-clad flashers and intoxicated frat boys. The rest of the year, it's a typical tourist destination—bars, hotels, restaurants. Palm trees, warm water. Fine white sand. Two hours from the poorest county in the nation, you can sip a seven-dollar margarita at the beachfront bar, and watch the sun bob messily into the waves.

After a two-hour drive, we got gelato in cones, walked down to the water. Except for a few late night strollers, the beach was abandoned. Araceli mashed the last of her gelato into her mouth, and made a beeline for the waves. She jumped in, splashing in swirling whitewater up to her shins. "It's warm!" she shouted, the wind whipping her hair around her face. I slipped off my flip-flops. The water buzzed, a warm cola at my feet.

"It's like a bath." Margo stood in the water up to her ankles, jeans rolled just below her knees.

I was used to the prickle of the Pacific. An ocean that turned arms to cold rubber, spat me back hollow, chilled. This water was like the womb. A nurturing broth. A place for pink, undeveloped souls to bob before they're born. I watched saltwater dampen the strings of my jean skirt, tangle them in foam. The moon was a bright shard. I stepped deeper into the water, soaking my skirt. The water was dark like liquor. When I slapped at foam, phosphorescent algae sparked with glints of fiery light.

September 15

I imagine myself sticking my hand into my ribcage, pulling out shards of colored glass, waving them under Philip's nose. "See, see?" I ask, shaking them slightly. "Do you see what's inside of me?"

I finally broke down and put the air conditioning on. I am imagining that this kills thousands of baby seal pups.

It would be nice if Philip were here to enjoy this air conditioning with me. Imagine: Instead of touching my arm and saying, "God, you're sweaty," he could say: "All of that colored glass you keep pulling out of your ribs would make a nice window, maybe in a church."

September 16

Janice hung around my desk again at lunch.

"What'd you do this weekend, miss?"

"My housemates and I went to South Padre Island."

"I love South Padre! I went there for Mardi Gras last year. I was in the back of the truck and this other truck of guys has some beads and I'm all, 'give me some,' and they throw one and then they're like, 'Now you have to show us something.' And I'm like, 'You're not seeing any of this, this, or *this*.' And they're like, 'You owe us!' And I'm like, 'The only thing you're seeing is *this*.'" She flips up her middle finger.

September 17

Bush leading by four percent. Let us sit down on the curb of the pavement and weep.

September 18

"You know what I had to scrub off a desk today?" I told Señora Gomez in the copy room. "ROBERTO RUIZ SUCKS BLACK COCK."

Señora Gomez sipped her coffee. "Sounds like Roberto is making some poor life choices."

I stood there for a moment, holding my files. "Your comment could be interpreted as both racist and homophobic."

"*Mija*," Senora Gomez said. "A 14-year old should not be sucking cock of any race, creed, color, or nationality."

"What's the age cut off?"

"How do you mean?"

"At what point is cock-sucking acceptable? 16? 18?"

"Ms. Freedman, this is sexual harassment in the workplace," Señora Gomez said, and walked out.

September 22

Conversation Between me and God:

Me: Hi. What's up?

God: Silence.

Me: So. I feel like I always end up talking about myself. Let's talk about you for a change.

God: Silence.

Me: What's on your mind?

God: My children and how they suffer.

Me: Oh. Right. I'll get on that.

September 28

In a punishing mood, I put on a baseball hat and earphones and an inch thick coat of sunscreen and went running on the track along the canal. I cranked the volume on my cd player, playing slit-your-wrists indie dissonance, sun glinting bright on my damp face, the exhaust from cars like the warm breath of lambs.

September 29

A low moan in my bones: I want to go home I want to go home.

October 1

Leaving campus at six P.M., saw Campos yanking kid (I am assuming her own) by the shirt into her car. He had a square of masking tape over his mouth.

October 2

Seven is God's perfect number, Amelia Basil informed me today. Who knew?

October 3

Janice Gibbs, on family: "Once, my dad's girlfriend pulled my hair. So I threw a cat at her. It landed on her back, and she was crying."

October 5

Painted in dust on the back of a van: *I wish my wife was this dirty.*
Message painted below it, in a different hand: *She is.*

October 6

Momentum trickling out like someone poked a hole in my foot. Lithium, I am going to flush you down the toilet.

October 7

Kristi, on family: "My dad is nothing to me. I've never met him. When I was in my mom's stomach he locked her in a room for two days with no food or water for lying to him. He asked her if she smoked his last cigarette, and she said no. After he let her out, she beat him up and left."

October 8

Cooked dinner. Garlic stinging under my fingernails. Hold it together, damn it. Hold it together.

October 10

Philip and I shared a pint of Ben & Jerry's and watched a special on a man with a face-eating tumor. It was followed up by a special about a resilient woman with no legs. She worked a job, married, and reared a baby. Legless. With a terrific attitude. She made me feel like shit.

October 11

Kristi, on neighbors: Our neighbors are Filipino and I hate them. Yesterday their dog got out and it started attacking our dog. "Why don't you go back to your own country," I said, "if you can't even take care of your dog?"

"I'll kill your dog," the man said.

"I'll kill you," I said. Then I started punching him and my mom had to tear me away so he didn't press charges. Then she gave me a beer to calm down, 'cuz when I start to fight people they press charges. So I just drank a bottle and then we went and had fun.

October 12

Bought sandwich cookies for parent teacher conference, set them out on flimsy paper plates.

Phil Gasher's Dad: *(Looking me over.)* I have concert T-shirts older than you.
Me: And I bet they're equally effective at classroom management.
Mr. Gasher: *(Blank look of confusion.)*
Me: Never mind.

October 13

Kristi and her posse populated my doorway after school.

Kristi: Have you heard the rumor?
Me: What rumor?
Kristi: People are saying that I'm pregnant.

Me: Are you?

Kristi: No.

Me: Um, well. Congratulations, then, I guess.

October 14

Andy Lopez: Miss? There's something I've been meaning to tell you.

Me: Yes?

Andy Lopez: Last week, I saw a dead rat.

Me: Okay.

Andy Lopez: Ants were coming out of its eyes.

Me: Thanks for letting me know.

October 15

First line in Phil Gasher's essay: *Saving lives is so amazing it will put a dent in your heart.*

October 16

Character Flaws:

*Fear that dogs will see into my soul and growl at me.

*Fear that babies will see into my soul and cry when I hold them.

*Fear, basically, that something is rotten at my core, and that people will see through to my rotten, shameful, center.

October 17

In college, Lakshmi's mother took us out to tea, and gently stroked my ear. "You have lucky earlobes," she said. She gazed at my collarbone. "But those moles around your neck could be a noose."

I thought of myself at 17, making a noose from an extension cord in the garage. My mother, swinging from a rafter. Why the garage, with these dark moments? Why always the garage?

October 18

Kristi stayed in the classroom during lunch, drawing on the back of a comma-splice worksheet.

"What's up, Kristi?"

"I'm pregnant."

I sat down beside her. "How are you feeling?"

"Bad. But kind of good, also. I don't know."

"Yeah?"

"I think I know what I'm gonna name it."

"Yeah?"

"Savannah."

She indicated her doodle.

Printed on it, in large block letters: SUFANA.

October 19

After dinner, Philip leaned into my doorway. "I have a present for you."

"What's the occasion?"

"Your first pregnant student!" He handed me a small plastic toy. "Think of it as a consolation prize. I found it in the Korean discount store."

It was a plastic snow globe depicting Christ's resurrection. Half the glitter water had leaked out. Christ was wading in it waist-deep, arms raised before his tomb. Bowing, golden-haired angels flanked him. When I shook it, the water frothed a little, the glitter spun. Plastic Jesus, drowning in a whirlpool bubble bath. A resurrection snow globe.

"You're trying to cheer me up with a tchotchke?"

Philip flopped on my bed. "I thought it was funny."

I turned it over, and squinted to read the tiny print. "*Made in Hong Kong.* God. This was probably made in a sweatshop."

"Yup."

I shook the snow globe. "And Jesus wept."

"Yeah, well. Merry Christmas."

October 20

Have not yet been able to heal and transform any kid in the deep and powerful way they needed to be healed and transformed.

Get on it, teacher-face.

October 21

When I walked outside to bring an empty milk jug to the recycling bin, I saw a ghost leaning over the dumpster, eating my thrown-away stew.

No. It was a homeless man. I slipped the milk carton into the trash. "Excuse me," I said. He grinned at me, teeth glinting in the moonlight.

October 22

I woke up covered in aches, wanting a full body massage. I realized I had no one who I could ask for one. And I felt so lonely I wanted to die.

October 30

Me: What are you going to be for Halloween?
Kristi: We're going as babies.
Me: Cute!
Angelica: I mean, that's what we're going as at school.
Kristi: At night we're going to be cheerleaders. We got knee-high boots.
Angelica: We're going to be hooker cheerleaders.
Kristi: *Dead* hooker cheerleaders.
Me: *(Pause.)* That seems inappropriate.

November 1

Two at a time, I climbed the stairs. My body felt itchy and achy. There was ringing in my ears. I ran the tub full of scalding water. If I cooked myself thoroughly, I could climb out of the tub unbroken. Whole.

After forty-five minutes, Philip knocked on the door. "Can I grab my toothbrush?"

"I don't care."

He opened the door. "Jesus, Laura, I thought you had the curtain pulled."

"These bubbles are protecting my modesty."

"Are you okay?"

"You're stressing me out with your invasive questions. Hand me my towel." I caught the ragged pink terrycloth, and stood up, wrapping it around myself.

"What's the matter?"

"All the shoes I like best are made for eight-year-old girls." I stood there, dripping.

He looked at me, bemused. "Yeah. Well. Tess and I broke up."

"We should take a walk."

November 2

I stumbled through my day like a drunken dreamer, flashes of the night lapping over my eyes—wavering weeds, sweet grass, warmth of skin on skin eclipsing the heat of an electric blanket. All day he was like a ghost on my skin. When I showered, I was sorry beads of water washed away his sweat.

November 5

I lie awake, watching his body. His body, like a moonscape in the darkness.

November 8

Not sleeping. I don't want to sleep. I want to crack open the cage of my ribs, scoop out my heart with an ice cream scooper, and stamp it on paper. So he can see: his name is written there. In blood! Ha ha! "Here, look!" I will say. And he will tape it to the fridge.

November 9

That fire inside me sprouting—my mind tingles, clicking at a hundred miles a minute. NOW I can speak to the children without fear. NOW I know what to say. Before I was dormant, a pile of ashes. Now, I'M ON FIRE.

November 12

I must wear pants/ When I go out/ Or they will shake their heads/ And shout: "Hey! Where are her pants?!"

November 18

Ordered leather-bound journals for all the kids. YES. Everyone deserves nice things, for once!!!

November 20

Idea: Jeopardy vocab game. ("VOCAB STAB!") Cardboard from dumpster! Industrial grade glitter glue!

November 22

Ordered 20 pounds of candy hearts custom printed to read: ENGLISH ROCKS! Because ENGLISH ROCKS!

November 23

Thanksgiving break. Philip in California w. fam. Kind of empty. Blank, dull, broken house.

November 24

Optimal life choice: not get out of bed. Ever. Until Philip comes back.

November 25

Philip called. Got back together with his girlfriend, apparently. Over break.

November 30

Stayed home again. Invisible ocean smacking me with waves.

December 1

My heart feels rubbed raw and tender, pulverized and soaked in vinegar.

December 2

There is a world of pain inside me. A profound terrain of hurt.

December 3

My birthday tomorrow. Amazing timing. Happy 23rd birthday, Laura Freedman. Once more you have failed at the most basic and human of tasks: maintaining a romantic relationship for over two weeks.

Jesus, help me to rally. Help me to wallow out of this sorrow. Cupcakes. I will make cupcakes for the class.

December 4

Cupcakes = bad call.

December 5

They are deviant trolls. Feral raccoons devoid of impulse control.

December 6

Why did I think I could do this? Why did I ever think I could do this?

December 7

There is pride in expecting too much from my stunted heart.

December 8

A dingy loudness. Rustling like the wings of sparrows. I keep turning around, thinking I hear creatures running behind me.

December 9

Isaiah 45:9 "The clay does not ask the potter: what are you making?"
Good Lord. Good Lord. What are you making?

December 11

Hurricane warnings went out over the radio this morning—the tail end of Mitch might slam us in its sweep over Northern Mexico. Shops laid sandbags on their stoops, and some merchants are nailing boards over windows. For now, though, the sky is hazy blue. A block from the convent, a truck pulls up to the curb, and a man beckons me to his car through the glinting screen.

December 12

Couldn't sleep. Went outside, lay down in the itchy, squelchy grass, listened to cicadas humming, watched low smears of pink clouds racing across a blue-black sky. The air smelled like taco stand and jasmine flowers. Tinkly music and rowdy yelling wavered over from the cantinas, and some kind of nocturnal birds were squalling from telephone wires or palm trees. The air was thickening in humidity, sign of a coming storm.

December 13

I lie on faded floral sheets, listen to rain lash against the window. The Rio Grande Valley isn't really a valley. It's an alluvial floodplain. When rain comes fast, the dry ground can't soak it up. Floods flash fast. It's devastating to the families in the *colonias* outside town, where electricity is rickety, water running scarce, where families of twelve share one trailer or tin-roofed hut.

I unhook the lock on the balcony screen door, step out into the wind. Hurricane-force gales whip the spindly palm trees on Main Street, thrashing their fronds, bending them back like slingshots. The sky is the shade of ash, smearing itself around unhappily. Thunder tears from its bolted chamber; sound waves ripple through the grass. The rain falls in torrents, in sheets. The temperature drops to frigid. My skirt and shirt plaster to my skin. Lightning streams and crackles: rough yellow, electric pink.

Below: abandoned streets. Rain surging down the gutters, sluicing into drains. Pouring now with fury and intention, dripping from eaves, hurling itself, gathering in angry pools along the sidewalks, filling the drains faster than they suck it down. The pale blue canals, I imagine, chortle brown. They soon will crumble, overflow, spill through.

I stand there with my hands on the balcony railing, fingers freezing white, toes going numb. I stand there. And I watch the waters rise.

✳ LIKE THE RUSSIAN SAID ✳

My sanitary pad heavy with blood, I stumble through the Public Cemetery of Plano. That baby gutted me. Two weeks, still bleeding. Still bloated in body, foggy of mind.

Olivia's grave is easy to find, as she is sitting on it.

"Laura." She drags on her cigarette. "Sit."

I ease down on the grave across from her. "They switched her at the hospital."

"Who, now, hon?"

I rub my scalp. "No one believes me."

"But you have such an honest face."

I cover my face with my hands.

"I warned you."

"I didn't believe you." I wipe my nose. "You can't trust ghosts."

"Oh no?"

"Like in *Hamlet*."

"I never got the chance to read much Shakespeare." She drains a ghostly can of Diet Rite, tosses it behind a bush.

"Hamlet's dad appears to him and says he was murdered by Hamlet's uncle. *Horrible, most horrible. Murder most foul.* Hamlet doesn't know whether to trust him."

"If you can't trust family, who can you trust?"

"That's the thing. The ghost might not be his father. It could be a demon, tempting him to mortal sin."

"I have signed no contract with the fallen one." She raises her left hand. "I do solemnly swear." She stands up. "Now which way do you want it?"

"What?"

She gives me a levelheaded stare.

"I'm not going to do what you did."

"Of course not. You don't have the spine. You'll do pills. Or gas."

"I don't have pills."

"Well, you've got a car, dear. You just need a garage. Or a hose."

I sift damp gravel through my fingers.

"Listen, the house is still empty. They haven't managed to sell it yet. You still have the key, right? It's waiting for you. Get back in the car, drive the five blocks, bam."

"Did you even want these?" I thrust out the roses.

She smells them. "A beautiful bouquet." She tucks it under her arm. "You're a thoughtful girl." She jerks her head to the side. "C'mon."

"I'll ruin Ben's life."

"Honey." She strokes my cheek. "You already did."

Ice cold globes of grapefruit in my chest.

" Stephen."

"Your brother won't mind. If you've lost a mother, you can lose a sister. Didn't a poet say that? '*The art of losing isn't hard to master*'?"

"That's not what she meant."

"Well. You're the one with the degree."

I lean against the hot metal of the car. "This is the worst thing you can do. The worst thing you can do to anyone."

"Believe me, you're doing that kid a favor. You want to end up drowning her in a bathtub?" Olivia wraps her arm around my waist. "Better yet, why don't you wait four years? Be a *good* mommy. Bake cookies with silver sprinkles. Paint a mural on her wall. Be that kid's best friend. Then have your ugly breakdown. Let her pound on the door while you cut at your wrists. Let her think she can *save* you."

I lay my hands over my still-pouchy stomach.

Olivia smoothes my hair. "You're the gun on the mantle, hon. Like the Russian said: You're going to go off."

It's just what happens next.

The garage is blisteringly hot. By the time I get the door closed, I am drenched in sweat. My thighs stick to the seat. I roll down the windows. Blast the air conditioning.

"Stop smoking."

"What does it matter now?"

I am starting to feel it: smog. Sweet oncoming sleep. But a minnow fights the current, pulling with unease.

"Where do I go?"

"Same place I went."

"You're *here*."

"No, no, honey, I'm in heaven. This is just—what do you call it—a temporal projection. A day trip. I'm here to give you safe passage. Ferry you across the Jordan." She unties the bouquet, weaving flower through stem, making a wreath, a crown. She sets it on my head. "I'm your ministering angel."

I stare at her woozily. "I think you're the devil."

She opens her pocketbook. Dabs her forehead with a pink cloth with scalloped edges. Sighs. "What does it matter now?"

"Get thee hence, Satan."

And she is gone.

✵ THE APPLE ✵

A woman served only herself, save this—once she gave an apple to a hungry girl. When she dies, the devils whisk her to the lake of fire, where she cries for mercy to her guardian angel. The angel speaks to God, who says: take that apple, see if it will pull her out of hell.

The angel extends the apple, the woman grabs hold, and—in a twist of grace—it yanks her from the flames. The woman cries out in relief. A smoldering soul grabs hold of her ankle. Another soul grabs that ankle, and so on, ad infinitum, until a whole chain of souls is flying up to heaven.

The woman sees linked souls looping behind her—her mother, choked by rose vines, pulls her father, chained with dangling stones. Souls latch on in infinite spire: cords of cowards, strings of sorcerers, helixes of heretics. The lustful dangle from the sullen; hoarders hang from wastrels. Up they fly: hypocrites and betrayers, liars and gluttons, murderers and sowers of discord.

At the end of the chain is the broken angel himself: lurched out of his ice. Clasping Judas's ankle. Sailing finally home.

She holds on: with all her heart, all her soul, all her might.

Hell is emptied.

Mercy has crept in.

The Iowa Short Fiction Award and the John Simmons Short Fiction Award Winners, 1970–2014

Donald Anderson
Fire Road

Dianne Benedict
Shiny Objects

Marie-Helene Bertino
Safe as Houses

Will Boast
Power Ballads

David Borofka
Hints of His Mortality

Robert Boswell
Dancing in the Movies

Mark Brazaitis
The River of Lost Voices: Stories from Guatemala

Jack Cady
The Burning and Other Stories

Pat Carr
The Women in the Mirror

Kathryn Chetkovich
Friendly Fire

Cyrus Colter
The Beach Umbrella

Jennine Capó Crucet
How to Leave Hialeah

Jennifer S. Davis
Her Kind of Want

Janet Desaulniers
What You've Been Missing

Sharon Dilworth
The Long White

Susan M. Dodd
Old Wives' Tales

Merrill Feitell
Here Beneath Low-Flying Planes

James Fetler
Impossible Appetites

Starkey Flythe, Jr.
Lent: The Slow Fast

Kathleen Founds
When Mystical Creatures Attack!

Sohrab Homi Fracis
Ticket to Minto: Stories of India and America

H. E. Francis
The Itinerary of Beggars

Abby Frucht
Fruit of the Month

Tereze Glück
May You Live in Interesting Times

Ivy Goodman
Heart Failure

Barbara Hamby
Lester Higata's 20th Century

Ann Harleman
Happiness

Elizabeth Harris
The Ant Generator

Ryan Harty
Bring Me Your Saddest Arizona

Mary Hedin
Fly Away Home

Beth Helms
American Wives

Jim Henry
*Thank You for Being
Concerned and Sensitive*

Lisa Lenzo
Within the Lighted City

Kathryn Ma
All That Work and Still No Boys

Renée Manfredi
Where Love Leaves Us

Susan Onthank Mates
The Good Doctor

John McNally
Troublemakers

Molly McNett
One Dog Happy

Tessa Mellas
Lungs Full of Noise

Kate Milliken
If I'd Known You Were Coming

Kevin Moffett
Permanent Visitors

Lee B. Montgomery
Whose World Is This?

Rod Val Moore
Igloo among Palms

Lucia Nevai
Star Game

Thisbe Nissen
*Out of the Girls' Room
and into the Night*

Dan O'Brien
Eminent Domain

Philip F. O'Connor
*Old Morals, Small Continents,
Darker Times*

Sondra Spatt Olsen
Traps

Elizabeth Oness
Articles of Faith

Lon Otto
A Nest of Hooks

Natalie Petesch
After the First Death
There Is No Other

Marilène Phipps-Kettlewell
The Company of Heaven:
Stories from Haiti

Glen Pourciau
Invite

C. E. Poverman
The Black Velvet Girl

Michael Pritchett
The Venus Tree

Nancy Reisman
House Fires

Josh Rolnick
Pulp and Paper

Elizabeth Searle
My Body to You

Enid Shomer
Imaginary Men

Chad Simpson
Tell Everyone I Said Hi

Heather A. Slomski
The Lovers Set Down Their Spoons

Marly Swick
A Hole in the Language

Barry Targan
Harry Belten and the
Mendelssohn Violin Concerto

Annabel Thomas
The Phototropic Woman

Jim Tomlinson
Things Kept, Things Left Behind

Doug Trevor
The Thin Tear in the Fabric of Space

Laura Valeri
The Kind of Things Saints Do

Anthony Varallo
This Day in History

Don Waters
Desert Gothic

Lex Williford
Macauley's Thumb

Miles Wilson
Line of Fall

Russell Working
Resurrectionists

Charles Wyatt
Listening to Mozart

Don Zancanella
Western Electric